The
FEARLESS
Birth Book

Dedicated to all of us – may we forever be growing, changing, and owning our power unapologetically.

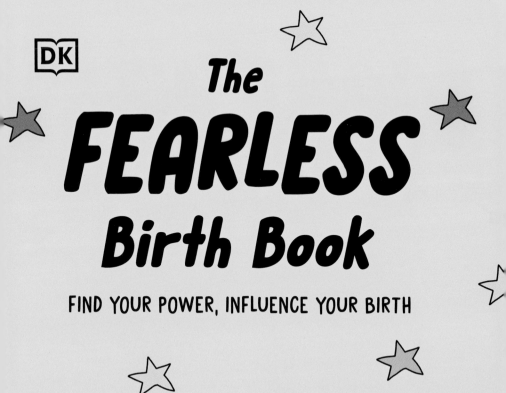

The
FEARLESS
Birth Book

FIND YOUR POWER, INFLUENCE YOUR BIRTH

Words and
illustrations by
**Emma
Armstrong**

CONTENTS

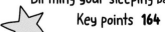

I am Emma Armstrong
Your birth bestie and fellow superhero Mum

Hi, I am Emma Armstrong. A mother of two gorgeous boys, a birth influencer, doula, and hypnobirthing practitioner. I've been working in the birth world for around five years now, after I lost my mum to cancer during my first pregnancy. Talk about timing, Mum! I am also an illustrator by accident and apparently now an author! I swear a lot. I don't always get to wash my face in the morning and I regularly juggle nappies, toys, and clothes. It just so happens that I'm pretty obsessed with birth, women, and girl power, and I can break down the boring, overwhelming stuff and make it fun, resonating, and palatable. I've taught hundreds of women and couples through my classes and supported births in person and virtually, worldwide. My bestselling course and flashcards have served over 40,000 of you and my community continues to grow, with over 160,000 and counting. Wowzers.

I've been through my fair share of shit, from body dysmorphia, anxiety, and depression to loss, grief, and anger, all of which operate from a level of fear. Fear operates on a low-frequency vibration, causing a negative energy that can breed limiting beliefs, closing the mind to alternative narratives and possibilities. So we basically miss ALL the good stuff.

These limiting beliefs, formed through past experiences or conditioning, are holding you back from realising your full potential. Your power lies in facing fear head on with compassion,

self-love, and determination. Becoming fearless doesn't mean forgetting about fear but rather mastering it and using it as a catalyst for personal growth and transformation. My mission is to reach as many of you as possible and pass you a little spark so that you may start your journey to reigniting the fire inside of you.

I am so passionate about your choices, your autonomy, and helping you look within so that you can emerge from the flames feeling like the fearless goddess I know you are. Which is why *The Fearless Birth Book* was born. See, I'm going to be honest. Birth is full of opinions, ideas, and bullshit, which breed FEAR and fuckery. But I don't care for the long-winded articles, 500-page textbooks, or Sharon down the road giving me advice about shitting a watermelon... Cue sarcasm. I care about your fears and how they're holding you back, limiting belief in yourself and your innate ability to birth. Fear is the root of a hell of a lot of problems. Not only does it manifest as anxiety, depression, and you not believing in yourself, but it also impacts your body through tension, oppression, and pain. This book is designed to gently guide you back to yourself so that you may release those fears, find yourself and your power, and feel confident about your body and birth. Call me your birth bestie, handing you all the tools, tricks, tips, and spark so you can go rule your birth like a queen.

The Journey

This is how it's going to go down. Are you ready?

BODY

Tuning into the power of your body autonomy, intuition, and how to work with it to create an enjoyable birth experience.

BRAIN

Facing the fears head on, self-acceptance, and reframing your brain for the ultimate aligned birth experience.

BABY & BEYOND

Embracing your transformation,
finding your mother magic,
and building a connection
with your baby.

BIRTH

Crafting your unique
birth vision, understanding
your options, and birthing like
a fearless goddess.

BRAIN

Reframing your brain for birth

For too long, women have been conditioned to feel shame about their bodies and their sexuality. If we can reprogram the brain, we can reprogram birth.

The role of the brain is often left on the sidelines, yet it deserves centre stage.

Your past and present experiences are the architects of your self-image and perspective on life. They dictate every second of your experience.

The way you are programmed

A lifetime of conditioning has left your brain feeling all sorts of ways! How did it get here and what does it mean?

From the moment you enter this wild world, your brain kicks into sponge mode, eagerly absorbing every tiny bit of information and experience that comes its way. It soaks up all the knowledge and experiences around you. But this sponge-like brain of yours isn't just passively taking it all in. Oh no! It's busy weaving together a complex web of beliefs, values, and thought patterns that will shape how you view yourself, others, and the entire world.

Your family dynamics, cultural and societal norms, educational systems, and the all-mighty media - they've all had their sticky fingers on the

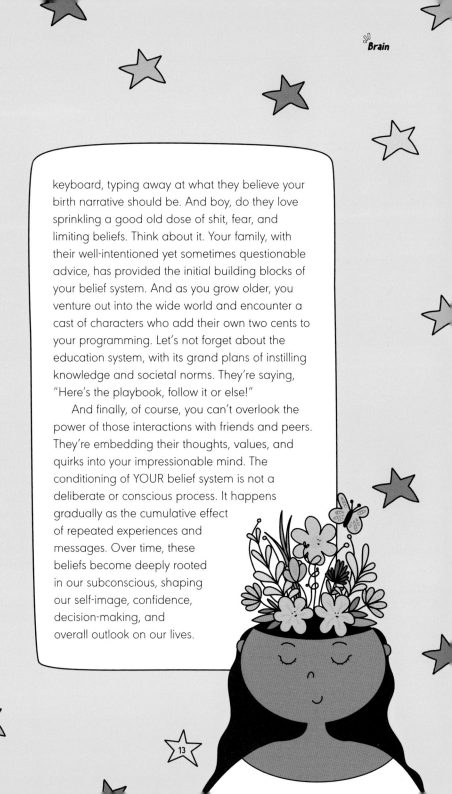

keyboard, typing away at what they believe your birth narrative should be. And boy, do they love sprinkling a good old dose of shit, fear, and limiting beliefs. Think about it. Your family, with their well-intentioned yet sometimes questionable advice, has provided the initial building blocks of your belief system. And as you grow older, you venture out into the wide world and encounter a cast of characters who add their own two cents to your programming. Let's not forget about the education system, with its grand plans of instilling knowledge and societal norms. They're saying, "Here's the playbook, follow it or else!"

And finally, of course, you can't overlook the power of those interactions with friends and peers. They're embedding their thoughts, values, and quirks into your impressionable mind. The conditioning of YOUR belief system is not a deliberate or conscious process. It happens gradually as the cumulative effect of repeated experiences and messages. Over time, these beliefs become deeply rooted in our subconscious, shaping our self-image, confidence, decision-making, and overall outlook on our lives.

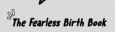

My story

When I was a child, ballet morphed from an enjoyable hobby into a serious pursuit, and competition was no longer fun but a realm of fierce rivalry. My mum, my biggest supporter, cheered me on, yet her encouragement to "do my best" didn't spare me the pressure to fit into a supposed aesthetic ideal. I was onstage with a smile that made my jaw ache, make-up that masked my real face, and hair pulled into a bun so tight it was borderline torturous. No joke: I remember the tears welling up in my eyes from the pain of having my hair brushed back, but there was no room for complaints in the quest for perfection.

As I grew, my body began to change – puberty hit like a tonne of bricks. I was sporting sticky-out boobs that filled me with self-consciousness, armpit hairs that I was absolutely not allowed to shave, and my body was a landscape of new, unfamiliar terrains. By the age of ten, dancing on pointe was a requirement, an experience that often left my toes bloody and me in agony. Yet, the pain was sold to us as a rite of passage – a sign we were "training" our bodies, tuning them like finely crafted instruments to reach ballerina perfection.

At the start of these early pre-teen years, body dysmorphia crept in, a monster that fed on my self-esteem.

My brain was programmed to believe in a distorted image of the "perfect" ballerina. My body was expected to be an ornament on display, performing flawlessly while never occupying too much space. This dysmorphia consumed me, fuelled a rebellion, and eventually led me down a dark path marked by anxiety, depression, alcohol and drug abuse, and toxic relationships with both men and women. My relationship with myself was perhaps the most damaging of them all. However, in 2017 something shifted. Engaging in selfless acts without the need to prove myself as "something or someone" sparked a change within me. I began journaling, sharing my experiences, and delving into my mind to truly understand my self-worth. It was during this process that things started falling into place.

Body dysmorphia crept in, a monster that fed on my self-esteem.

Self-acceptance

Imagine being comfortable and confident with your unique self! This is the first step to feeling confident about your body, birth, and choices.

Your past experiences have crafted your self-image and perspective on life. Your subconscious conditioning is calling the shots during birth. So how you feel about yourself and what you believe isn't just important, it's pivotal! That's where this book comes in.

The road to self-love is tough, and it's especially tough when you are feeling emotional and tired, with a changing body. But taking small steps to appreciate your incredible self, growing a baby and providing them with a safe home, will make changes for the better. A great way to start truly believing how special you are is to use affirmations DAILY. Practise reading them out loud. After a while those messages will start imprinting inside your subconscious mind.

As a thriving woman in my mid-thirties, I can look back now and say with certainty that I've grown into my skin, embraced my flaws, and made peace with my past, but the journey here was not smooth.

Tip: *Say this to yourself daily: I am beautiful just as I am. My unique self is worthy of love, confidence, and happiness.*

16

"After preparing myself
I didn't feel anxious at all
for birth. Either way, the
baby has to come out, can't
stay there forever!"

Why can't I get over it?

Emotional trauma is an intense psychological response in our brain when something or someone threatens your sense of safety and well-being.

Imagine your brain as this big-ass forest filled with winding paths and hidden trails. Each track represents a different stage of your life, experiences literally stamped into your mind from childhood through adolescence and adulthood. Some of these paths may have thorny bushes, fallen trees, and unexpected obstacles that have left a mark on you. As you go along your journey of pregnancy and birth, it's essential to reflect on the pathways you've already travelled. Are there some that have become overgrown with self-doubt or tangled with negative beliefs? Or others may be completely riddled with anxiety and stress. What emotional traumas are you holding on to? Let's see if we can illuminate some paths with self-discovery and power. By exploring the various pathways of the past and

REMINDER
Emotional trauma manifests differently in everyone. Our individual experiences, resilience, and support networks significantly affect how we handle these events. The key is recognising the signs of emotional trauma and seeking help when needed.

clearing away the shitty emotional undergrowth, you can create new, empowering trails that lead to growth, resilience, and self-acceptance. It's about forging new paths, ones that align with your true essence and allow you to navigate birth's twists and turns with confidence and grace. You can choose which directions to follow and which to let go of. By consciously tending to your emotional landscape, you can transform your forest of experiences into a sanctuary of self-love and personal growth. Let's venture into the depths of your forest. Discover hidden pathways that shape your sense of self, untangle and release the shit that no longer serves you. Embrace the incredible healing power of self-reflection, forgiveness, and self-compassion, as you create a new narrative that leads to a more authentic, fulfilling you!

What's going on in my brain?

Trauma can have profound effects on the brain, reshaping its structure and impacting various regions involved in how you think, decision-making, emotion, memory, and stress response. Here's a glimpse into how:

Prefrontal cortex

Trauma can actually make this important area of your brain shrink. This can lead to difficulties in managing emotions, coping with stress, and making decisions. For more see p.26.

Amygdala

The emotional centre of the brain. Can become overactive after trauma. This heightened sensitivity to fear and stress may lead to hyper-vigilance and a state of constant alertness.

Hippocampus

AKA the brain library. Crucial for memory and learning, but may also shrink in response to trauma. This can result in memory problems and difficulty processing and integrating traumatic experiences.

EFT TAPPING AND BREATHWORK ARE GREAT PRACTICES THAT MIGHT HELP YOU.

Tap into your playful side with brain buzzers for relaxation (p.44).

Childhood

Ah, remember when finger painting was the day's most important task? Childhood, with all its wonder and whimsy, also sets the stage for who you grow into. Our parents or caregivers, despite mostly having our best interests at heart, may have been dealing with their own baggage. Their own unresolved traumas can unknowingly influence us, shaping our behaviours and self-perception. Especially if your early years were full of hardships like neglect, a turbulent home life, or even abuse – it can dent your sense of self-worth and emotional fortitude.

But do not fear if this is you! The first step towards healing is understanding how childhood hardships and your parents' struggles have affected you and how you can heal this.

The teenage years

In the wild and often confusing world of adolescence, each day is a new ride on the rollercoaster of life. During this crazy phase, you're not only juggling body changes and hormonal surges but also wrestling with your identity and self-image. It's a time when we're exploring our boundaries, forming relationships, and making choices that can significantly impact our emotional landscape. Relationships in our teens can feel like a high-stakes game of tag. These connections, whether friendships, family dynamics, or first loves, can leave lasting impressions. They can shape our expectations for future relationships, impact our self-worth, and influence our emotional patterns. For example, a toxic friendship or heart-wrenching break-up could seed anxieties or fears that we carry forward.

Adulthood

And then you're an adult or "supposed to be". A lot of us as young adults may suddenly carry the burdens of the world: waves of relationships, peers, past traumas, and experiences. Every wave, whether a tiny ripple or a colossal tsunami, has its impact. It shapes your journey and how you perceive the imminent adventure of birth. Yet, there's an undercurrent of hope that pervades your story. As a voyager on the sea of life, you're not helpless against the waves. You have the power to understand these experiences, chart your course, weather the storms, and emerge like the resilient badass you are. Like the sea ebbs and flows, you, too, can work on these past experiences, transforming them from overwhelming waves into gentle, neutral memories.

Who are you? Really

Just imagine: You're looking in the mirror and thinking, "Who the hell am I?" It's a question that takes courage, curiosity, and some serious sass to peel back the layers and get to the core of your self. But here's the thing: knowing the REAL you isn't about fitting into some predetermined mould or living up to society's expectations. It's about embracing your quirks, flaws, and unique essence. It's about chucking away the masks and shaking off the expectations. It's about exploring the nooks and crannies of your soul, diving deep into the sea of emotions, and unleashing the unapologetic badass within.

It's time for you to shine! Turn to page 32 to reframe your brain.

But how do you know when you've found the REAL you?

You'll know you've found the real you when you're living life on your terms, without the need for validation or approval from others. It's about embracing your wants and dreams, even if they seem unconventional to others. It's about honouring your values and staying true to your principles, even when the world tries to push you off course. When you've discovered the real you, there's a sense of deep inner peace and self-acceptance. Surround yourself with people who uplift and support you. Find your group of like-minded souls who see and celebrate the realness within you.

Don't panic if you're not quite there! It takes a lot to get to that point and the best part is that the REAL you is a work in progress and ever evolving. It's a long journey of self-discovery. It's about embracing change, learning from mistakes, finding the magic in moments, and embracing the messy, beautiful process of becoming.

When you've discovered the REAL you, there's a sense of deep inner peace and self-acceptance.

Self-acceptance and relationships

Here are some examples of how self-acceptance can be recognised within a relationship.

The real you in relationships

Ever felt the need to fake an orgasm or suppress the truth about your pleasure for the sake of a partner? It's more common than you might think. Many of us wear this mask of satisfaction to protect our partners, but in doing so, we lose a bit of ourselves. Let's drop the mask and make room for honesty and self-acceptance. If you are an introvert this is food for thought: it might be harder to feel confident during your labour and birth, so practicing to remove doubt might be helpful for your birth experience.

Knocking down bathroom barriers

Let's talk about those bathroom trips, like using the toilet or passing wind in front of your partner. If the idea of letting out a burp or discussing poo with your partner makes you cringe, it might be worth exploring why. If it's something you can't ever surpass, think how you can ensure privacy in the birth room so that you don't get any "cringe" moments sprung on you that send your brain into overdrive!

The pleasure principle

Self-pleasure is often swaddled in guilt and embarrassment. But it is NOT SHAMEFUL! Self-pleasure is a natural, empowering part of our sexuality. How does it make you feel? Flip the script and see it as a celebration of your body and desires. It's a beautiful way to understand your own body and what you truly need to feel pleasure, something that's incredibly beneficial for tapping into our power, understanding our intimate bits, and having body autonomy.

Body confidence = birth confidence

Here's where it all ties together. Even though it's likely that you won't give a shit about being naked in the birth room, deep in the love of labour, earlier on if you do feel uncomfortable or are not feeling confident, in or out of your attire, it may create unnecessary tension or stress during birth. The more you can work on that self-acceptance, body love, and open communication, the more likely you are to enjoy and feel good about your experience.

Let your birth experience be a testament to your power, confidence, and self-acceptance.

You're in control

The act of giving birth can be a truly empowering and incredible experience. And it starts with nurturing self-confidence and self-acceptance. So let's ditch societal expectations, embrace self-pleasure, and knock down those barriers of discomfort. You are more than capable of celebrating your body, your choices, and your strength. Let your birth experience be a testament to your power, confidence, and self-acceptance. Remember, you're the captain of your own ship and your birth experience can be as empowering and beautiful as you choose to make it. You've got this!

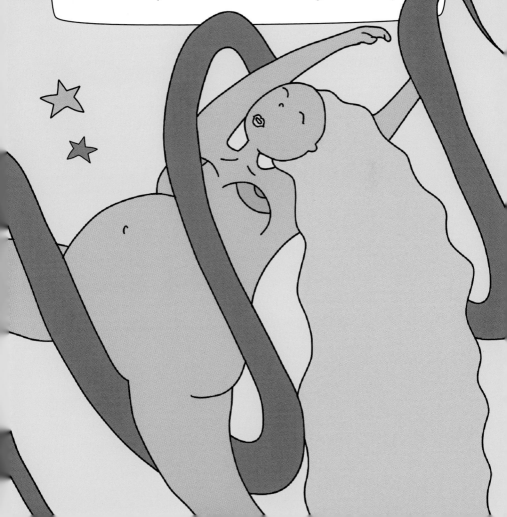

Brain and body connection

Welcome to the mind-blowing realm of the brain-body connection, where the real magic happens in a series of signals, changes, and damn good conversations. Get ready to take a trip through the mind's neural highways and the body's hormonal rollercoasters, where every twist and turn shapes the exhilarating ride of pregnancy and birth.

1 Prefrontal cortex

The prefrontal cortex, known as the "thinking brain", is responsible for decision-making, planning, and problem-solving. It plays a role in guiding choices and making informed decisions during birth.

THESE PARTS OF THE BRAIN ARE INVOLVED IN A MOTHER'S FIGHT-OR-FLIGHT RESPONSE WHEN CARING FOR HER YOUNG.

6 Pituitary gland

Receives signals from the hypothalamus to release oxytocin into the bloodstream, which stimulates uterine contractions during labour.

2 Hippocampus

The brain's memory centre helps store and retrieve our experiences. It weaves together the threads of our memories. This remarkable structure not only helps us tap into good memories during birth, but also has the ability to create new neutral and positive conditioning for birth.

3 Hypothalamus

Produces oxytocin, the hormone responsible for initiating contractions and facilitating the progress of labour. Oxytocin also promotes bonding between the mother and baby.

4 Amygdala

Processes emotions and triggers the fight-or-flight response. During birth, calming techniques and creating a supportive environment can help keep the amygdala in check.

5 Sensory cortex

The sensory cortex processes sensory information from the body, including pain signals. It interprets and relays sensations from the uterus, cervix, and birth canal to the brain, contributing to the overall experience of labour.

Your marvellous nervous system

Two branches of the nervous system handle the bodily processes you don't have to think about, like your heart beating, digestion, and breathing. These BFFs keep each other in check. The sympathetic nervous system is a network of nerves that helps your body activate its "fight, flight, or freeze" response. The parasympathetic nervous system is all about "rest and digest", helping you slow your heart rate. During birth, this balance is super important. When you feel safe, supported, and relaxed, the parasympathetic system takes over, triggering the release of oxytocin. It helps labour move along smoothly. If you're feeling anxious, the sympathetic system may try to take over, which can create a stress response and cause discomfort.

Pain and your brain

Fear impacts how we feel pain and how our body reacts to it. But, with understanding, reframing, and surrendering to it, you may just have an enjoyable, even pain-free birth experience!

So the previous section on self-acceptance and calming hormones sounded like a frickin' dream right... but what about the pain, I hear you cry? Fear not, my gorgeous goddess! We're not talking about pain with danger, but more, pain with purpose. The sensation of pain plays a big role in guiding your body's responses during the intricate ballet of birth. It's not a villain, but a messenger, communicating vital cues to your brain, nudging it to release oxytocin to power your contractions and prompting the surge of bliss-inducing endorphins. It even acts as a protective shield, signalling when to ease off the pushing or switch up your position to sidestep any tearing.

It's key to understand that pain isn't crafted in the muscles or nerves, but rather in the master control room itself – the brain. Now, before you raise an eyebrow, let me assure you that this doesn't make your pain any less real. Your brain is the artist that meticulously paints the sensation of pain your body feels. Just like any masterpiece, pain is influenced by an array of factors, emotion being a notable one. Your feelings can

intensity of each contraction, it's similar to pushing through the fatigue and ache you might feel while running. Just like a jog or a run, your muscles work hard and may tire, but you continue because you know deep down that it's okay. You trust your body's ability to handle the challenge, knowing that the discomfort is a necessary part of the journey. Just as a runner pushes through the miles, fuelled by determination and a goal in mind, you persevere through each contraction, guided by the knowledge that it brings you closer to meeting your precious baby. Each contraction is a step forward, a sign that your body is doing its incredible work of birthing new life. And just like running, where you find moments of respite and relief along the way, you'll experience the same during labour. The pauses between contractions give you a chance to catch your breath, gather your strength, and prepare for the next surge. These moments of rest are a reminder that you are strong, capable, and ready to conquer whatever lies ahead.

orchestrate physical changes: think of how fear or anger can prompt your muscles to tense up. This rings particularly true during labour. The fear of venturing into the unknown, confronting something potentially intense and intimidating, can lure us down a winding path of prolonged labour, heightened pain, and even trauma. Understanding this connection between mind and body offers us a powerful tool. By managing our fears and anxieties, we can influence our perception of pain and potentially transform our birthing experience.

Labour is a marathon

Imagine you're on a big run, heading towards the finish line of an exhilarating marathon. With each step, your leg muscles engage and tense, propelling you forward. It's like your uterus during contractions, a powerhouse of muscles working together to bring your baby into the world. As you push through the

It's normal to feel fear

By acknowledging fear, attending to it with curiosity, and reframing your perspective, you can create a powerful and influential experience.

Fear can be a tricky companion, manifesting in ways that affect our experience of pain. Sometimes, we may not even realise that fear is lurking beneath the surface, but its presence can be detected through certain clues. One is preoccupation, when our thoughts become fixated on the fear of the pain we anticipate. The desire to make pain "go away" can inadvertently reinforce the notion that pain itself is dangerous. By shifting our mindset, we can change the way our brain processes the sensations of pain and fear. Instead of resisting and wanting to eliminate the pain, we can acknowledge the sensation and practise leaning into it rather than trying to fight against it. By accepting the sensation as a neutral experience, we can literally change the way it feels to us. Trust in your body's wisdom and its ability to navigate this transformative process with strength and resilience.

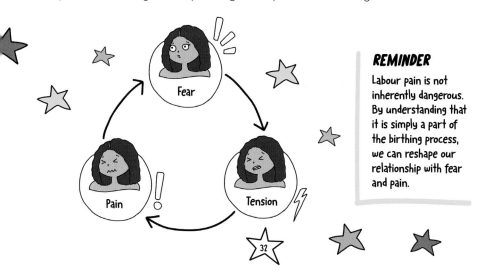

REMINDER

Labour pain is not inherently dangerous. By understanding that it is simply a part of the birthing process, we can reshape our relationship with fear and pain.

Brain

Things that can increase how PAIN feels

1. Fear = tension
2. Lack of understanding
3. Loss of control
4. Restricted movement
5. Tiredness/fatigue

Things that can decrease how PAIN feels

1. Confidence
2. Understanding/reframing
3. Support & autonomy
4. Movement
5. Breathing + floppy face, floppy fanny techniques

Go to page 92 to find out about the floppy face, floppy fanny technique.

Reframing the brain

You feel what you think! Understanding your brain is just giving you what you want is the starting point to interrupting those shitty thought patterns and creating a positive mindset.

Did you know that your brain is a bigger diva than a popstar on a world tour? Out of the 11 million pieces of information it receives per second, it only bothers to deal with about 40 of them. Who's allowing people into the VIP section? The reticular activating system, or RAS. It's the burly security guard of your brain, ensuring it's not flooded with more info than it can handle. The RAS is a mood reader. If your initial thoughts about birth are coated in fear, anxiety, or anger, your RAS will serve a buffet of those things.

This means you get stuck in a dizzying merry-go-round of stress. So, if your mental playlist keeps repeating, "Birth is scary, dangerous, and something to dread", guess what? Your brain will amplify it. That's why we can't let the brain be the forgotten audio tech when it comes to birth.

Your brain is your biggest fan
Whether having a C-section, planning a home birth, or embarking on any other path, your brain is already on board with your choice. Here's the

The brain is wired to support what you want. Regardless of whether it's fact or fiction.

34

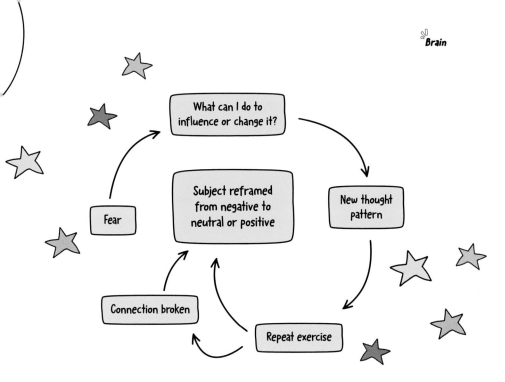

thing, babe: the brain is wired to support what you want. It's like having a fan club rooting for you regardless of whether it's fact or fiction. When you've already decided, your brain goes into overdrive, actively seeking information and evidence that aligns with your decision.

This phenomenon is known as confirmation bias. Your brain selectively filters information, favouring evidence that supports your assumptions. It's like putting on a pair of tinted glasses that enhance the colours of what you want to see, filtering out the rest. Your brain isn't intentionally deceiving you. It's just trying to create a seamless storyline that aligns with your thinking.

While this can be a powerful tool to reinforce your confidence and commitment, it's important to be aware of the potential pitfalls. When you're focused on confirming what you already know, you may close yourself off to other possibilities, missing out on valuable insights and alternative options that could broaden your perspective. And if we miss things, being unprepared can lead us down a path of trauma due to being surprised or out of control. Let's deep dive into the fascinating world of perception, memory, and emotional connections to discover how reframing can be our secret weapon during pregnancy, birth, and beyond.

The power of reframing

When we engage in reappraisal or reframing, we invite our brain to work magic. The process begins in to the left side of the brain which starts to silence the amygdala leading to less negative responses or thinking and allowing for more positive emotions to filter through. Let's break down these fancy scientific terms. Reappraisal is like putting on a new pair of glasses to see a situation from a different perspective. It's about shifting the lens through which you view the world, allowing you to find alternative meanings, silver linings, and hidden opportunities in even the most challenging circumstances. When you engage in reappraisal, the left prefrontal cortex lights up like a vibrant disco ball, showering your brain with a dazzling array of positive neurotransmitters. It's like throwing a party in your mind. Imagine the power of this transformation. Reframing a negative experience can change your emotional response, diffuse stress, and cultivate a positive outlook. It's like turning a frown into a smile, a cloud into a rainbow, or a stumble into a dance move – a superpower within you, waiting to be unleashed.

Processing

"I had **THE FEAR**, but I
continually focused on my
positive mindsets, and
reframing the brain kept me
in control of my breathing
and anxiety."

Enter the brain library...

Step into the mind-blowing, mind-bending world of the hippocampus, or as I affectionately call it, the brain library. Here you'll find a wealth of memories, emotions, and connections. It's like a vast archive of experiences that have shaped who you are today. Within its intricate network of neurons, the hippocampus stores and retrieves information related to events, people, places, and emotions. As you wander through the aisles of the brain library, you'll come across memories of joyful moments, accomplishments, and cherished relationships. These memories can evoke feelings of happiness, love, and gratitude, reminding you of the beauty and positivity in your life. However, alongside the pleasant memories, you may also stumble upon more challenging experiences. The hippocampus holds onto moments of happiness and joy, or moments of pain, trauma, or fear, which can trigger emotions of anxiety, sadness, or stress. These memories are a part of your story, but they don't define your future. An amazing thing about the brain library, and the brain itself, is its neuroplasticity. It has the capacity to rewire and reshape itself, allowing you to reframe the narratives stored within.

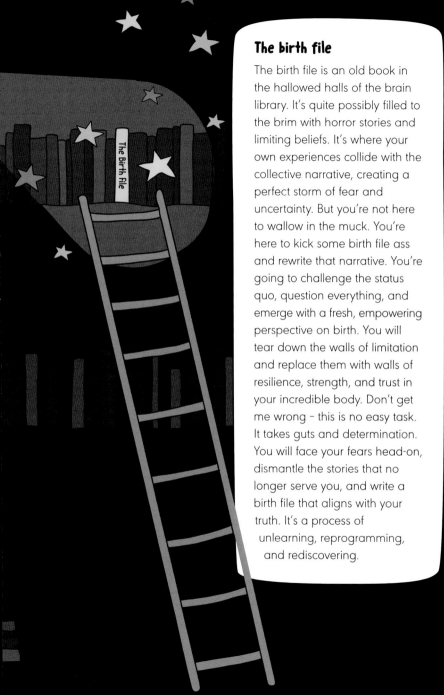

The birth file

The birth file is an old book in the hallowed halls of the brain library. It's quite possibly filled to the brim with horror stories and limiting beliefs. It's where your own experiences collide with the collective narrative, creating a perfect storm of fear and uncertainty. But you're not here to wallow in the muck. You're here to kick some birth file ass and rewrite that narrative. You're going to challenge the status quo, question everything, and emerge with a fresh, empowering perspective on birth. You will tear down the walls of limitation and replace them with walls of resilience, strength, and trust in your incredible body. Don't get me wrong – this is no easy task. It takes guts and determination. You will face your fears head-on, dismantle the stories that no longer serve you, and write a birth file that aligns with your truth. It's a process of unlearning, reprogramming, and rediscovering.

Reframing the birth file

It's time to face the music, babe... We're about to unleash some serious magic to neutralise the shitstorm and reclaim our power. Let's open up that birth file and start unpacking the shit. I want you to let out everything that comes to your mind about birth. We're going to explore the good, the bad, and the ugly, and find ways to reframe and neutralise the heck out of it.

The good: Take a moment to reflect on the positive aspects of birth that you've experienced or heard about. Maybe it's moments of empowerment, strength, love, or joy. If you don't have any, that's okay. This isn't a competition, it's more about understanding your unique space. Write down powerful statements that affirm the positive aspects and repeat them daily. Let them sink into your being, reinforcing these beliefs and recognising the incredible strength within you.

EXAMPLE: "The feeling when my baby is in my arms". How can you make this even more vivid in your mind? Write down your feelings.

You've got the power to reclaim control and navigate your birth experience on your terms.

The bad: This is the shitty stuff. The myths, false facts, or pointless "advice" that have been cluttering your mind. You're now going to throw them all away. They're useless, untrue, and hold no value. It's time to challenge and dismiss them, replacing them with evidence-based and empowering truths. You deserve accurate information and the confidence that comes with it.

EXAMPLE: "It's like shitting out a watermelon". FALSE. Look at the facts: a perineum isn't like a bum hole and a baby's head isn't like a watermelon.

The ugly: This is the stuff lurking in the birth file that's really causing havoc. It might be a past trauma or deeply programmed belief. Let's shine a light on those fears and break them down one by one. Take, for example, the fear of losing control. By educating yourself about the birth process, discussing your desires and concerns with your birth team, and incorporating relaxation techniques, you can regain a sense of control. You've got the power to reclaim control and navigate your birth experience on your terms.

EXAMPLE: "I'm going to be helpless". Create a spider diagram, mapping out all the factors contributing to this fear. Then write down ways that you can fight that fear.

REMINDER
Babe, this is your journey, and you're in the driver's seat. You're not alone, either. You are fierce, you are capable, and you've got what it takes to rock this birth like the goddess you are.

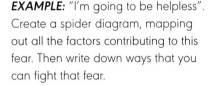

Hollywood has been talking shit

While we all love a good blockbuster, how birth has been shown in movies and TV shows has truly fucked with us!

It's almost as though every director in Hollywood held a meeting and decided, "Let's portray birth as the most terrifying, painful, and dramatic

Learn more about forced pushing, and why to avoid it, on page 103.

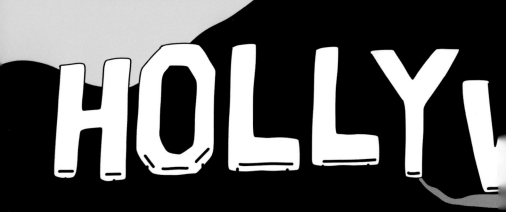

event of a woman's life!" Every movie birth seems to involve screaming women, panic-stricken partners, and doctors rushing in with forceps and alarmed expressions. These scenes have not only deeply embedded the idea of birth as a horrifying ordeal but also fostered a culture of fear and anxiety around this natural process. We must debunk these cinematic myths and reclaim the narrative around birth, returning it to the beautiful, empowering, and awe-inspiring event that it truly is. Because let's face it, Hollywood might know how to entertain us, but it's hardly the expert on birth!

Brain buzzers

 Brain buzzers are sensations that trigger positive memories and emotions associated with specific experiences. Sight, sound, smell, taste, and touch have a profound effect on our state of mind. Build your own unique toolkit of feel-good buzzers that you can tap into during labour and birth.

Touch

The sensation of a hug, a reassuring touch, or the texture of something comforting like your fave blanket, can ignite a world of emotions within you. Your brain is hardwired to remember the power of touch and respond with a flood of feel-good chemicals that make you feel safe, loved, and utterly blissful.

1. Your fav pillow or blanket
2. Massage
3. Your most comfy clothes
4. Holding hands
5. Loving touch

Sight

Just one glance at a familiar object, a beloved photograph, or a meaningful symbol can transport you back to a moment that gives you that warm, fuzzy feeling. It's like hitting the rewind button in your brain and reliving those joyful memories all over again.

1. Cherished photographs
2. Vision board
3. Sentimental items
4. Nature and people
5. Inspiring images or quotes

Brain

Sound

The familiar melody of a beloved song, the sound of laughter, or even the gentle hum of nature can evoke a rush of positive emotions. It's like your brain is conducting a symphony of happiness, tapping into the power of sound to create an uplifting experience.

1. Music
2. Rain
3. Voice notes
4. Silence
5. White noise

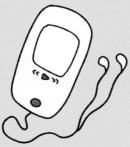

Smell

Scent has this incredible ability to bypass all other senses and take a shortcut to your brain's memory vault. It's like a direct line to the hippocampus, babe! The good old brain library.

1. Aromatherapy
2. Scents of nature
3. Comforting familiarities
4. Scented mementos
5. Perfume

Taste

The flavours that tantalise your taste buds, the comfort of a favourite treat, or the memories associated with a special meal can trigger a flood of pleasurable sensations. Just one bite or sip can transport you to a moment of pure bliss, igniting a spark of joy within you.

1. Birthday cake
2. Vanilla ice cream
3. Homemade soup
4. Herbal tea
5. Your fave meal

 A meaningful symbol can transport you back to a moment that gives you that warm, fuzzy feeling.

Practice makes perfect

By consistently practising sense-affirming exercises, you reinforce these positive associations in your brain, making them readily accessible during labour and birth. It's like training your brain to automatically create a sense of calm, confidence, and happiness whenever you need it!

Step 1: Choose your brain buzzer

Think about what makes your heart sing and your spirit soar. Trust your intuition and go with what resonates with your soul. This brain buzzer will become your secret weapon in unlocking your inner strength and relaxation during birth.

Step 2: Associate the brain buzzer

Now it's time to create a powerful connection between your brain buzzer and a state of deep relaxation. Practise touching or looking at your brain buzzer during a relaxation session or just before bed, focusing on the positive feelings and sensations it evokes. Add music to double up!

Step 3: Reinforce with repetition

Repetition is the key to building a strong brain buzzer. Consistently use your brain buzzer in your relaxation practice. Say your chosen phrase, listen to your song, or hold your brain buzzer object while visualising a peaceful and empowering birth. The more you reinforce this connection, the stronger and more effective your brain buzzer becomes.

Step 4: Create multi-sensory magic

Naked Doula-style, let's kick things up a notch! Engage all your senses to enhance the power of your brain buzzer. Combine soothing visuals, calming scents, gentle touch, and even relaxing sounds to create a multi-sensory experience that amplifies your brain buzzer's impact. The more you engage your senses, the deeper your state of relaxation and focus.

Step 5: Believe in the magic

Your mindset plays a crucial role in the effectiveness of your brain buzzers. Believe wholeheartedly in the power of your brain buzzer to bring you calm, comfort, and strength during childbirth. Trust in yourself and know that you have the ability to create your own magical birthing experience.

Oxytocin is queen bee

Here's all the ways this magical hormone will be buzzing through birth, from the warm-up to warming cuddles with your newborn.

Late pregnancy

In late pregnancy, it's theorised that your baby's lungs release a protein that acts like a hormone to trigger the onset of labour, giving the green light to kickstart the action. Meanwhile, your body is getting ready for the big moment. It's like a backstage crew working their magic. Progesterone which prevents premature labour is deactivated by increased oestrogen and maternal cortisol, allowing oxytocin, the love hormone, to rise and start preparing your uterus for some show-stopping contractions.

The start of labour

As those beautiful surges start, your baby's position and movements in the womb don't go unnoticed. The sensory nerves in the uterus and cervix are quick to catch the vibes and send a message back to your brain. Now, here's where the magic

happens. Your brain receives the signal and ramps up the production of oxytocin. Oxytocin is like the conductor of the orchestra. It cues the uterine muscles to start their rhythmic waves. Endorphins cling on to the end of your nerve receptors, blocking pain signals and making things feel a lot more

OXYTOCIN IS ALWAYS PRESENT IN LABOUR.

manageable. It's like the perfect symphony, each cycle bringing your baby one step closer to making their debut. BUT if something interrupts the flow of that oxytocin loop then things may slow down, change, or stop altogether. Put your foot down about stressful interactions to protect your oxytocin.

REMINDER

If you always come back to the queen oxytocin in every scenario during labour, you're more likely to avoid unwanted interventions.

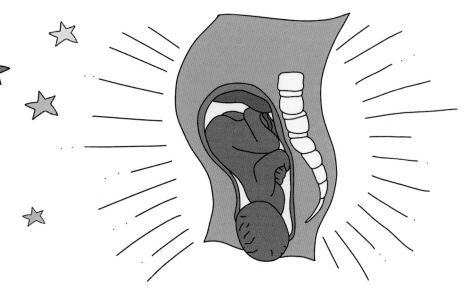

Birth

As your baby takes its wondrous voyage through your birth canal, it's like a little navigator, signalling to your body what it needs to do during labour. Imagine that with each movement and change in position, your baby whispers to your body, saying, "Hey, this way, a little more to the left, a gentle nudge here." It's like a secret language that guides you to navigate the final stages of labour. But the adventure doesn't stop there. Once your baby has triumphantly made their entrance into the world, a magical moment awaits. It's time for that first precious skin-to-skin contact. This magical connection triggers a flood of oxytocin. It's a signal to the uterus that says, "Hey, time to wrap things up!" This incredible hormone prompts the uterus to contract, helping to expel the placenta and reduce postpartum blood loss. It's nature's brilliant plan to ensure the mother's well-being and recovery after the awe-inspiring act of giving birth.

Skin-to-skin contact with your baby triggers a flood of oxytocin.

After the birth

After the moving arrival of your little one, the feedback loop between you and your baby keeps the magic alive. As you hold your precious bundle close in that tender skin-to-skin embrace, something extraordinary happens. The power of oxytocin surges through your body once again, as if saying, "Hey, it's time for milk! Let's make this breastfeeding journey a success!" This incredible hormone promotes milk let-down, ensuring that your little one receives the nourishment they need while deepening the unbreakable bond between you. But the feedback loop doesn't stop there.

Your baby, in their unique way, communicates with you through their cries, their feeding patterns, and even their little snoozes. It's like they have a secret code that only you can decipher. Their cues, their needs, and their rhythms influence your behaviour and responses as a parent. When your baby cries, it's their way of saying, "Hey, I need you. Comfort me, nourish me, love me." And you, being the amazing mama that you are, instinctively respond with tenderness and care. As you feed your baby and witness their contentment, it builds that connection and bond between you.

Individualised hypnobirthing

You may have heard that hypnobirthing can help you have a smooth and fear-free birth. It can, but it must be tailored to your unique needs.

A revolution in birth power

Standard hypnobirthing has been a beacon of hope for many of us expecting mums. It's a globally recognised technique that's been utilised across various cultures and societies worldwide. This method equips you with breathing exercises, self-hypnosis, and relaxation techniques to help you manage the discomfort and fear that can accompany childbirth. BUT, hypnobirthing can sometimes assume that we are all the same and can disregard the intricacies of personal experiences. While the method is based on broad, scientifically-backed principles, its effectiveness can vary greatly among individuals. This is largely because these standard practices don't necessarily resonate with everyone's unique neurological and emotional patterns. They may not consider your

Individualised hypnobirthing equips you with bespoke techniques to help you manage discomfort and fear.

specific past traumas, personal fears, or individual mental states, which are significant influencers in how you perceive and manage pain.

Your unique brain

The human brain is a masterpiece, a complex tapestry of experiences, emotions, and knowledge. Each one is different, sculpted by personal history and experiences. Your brain's established thought patterns, influenced by societal, familial, and personal beliefs about childbirth, may also add another layer of complexity to how you approach and experience birth. This is why a singular method like standard hypnobirthing may not work optimally for everyone. It simply can't cater to these unique and nuanced neurological landscapes.

Individualised hypnobirthing: the future of birth empowerment

This is where individualised hypnobirthing takes centre stage. It's not just about teaching you the

standard techniques; it's also about aligning these techniques with your unique emotional and psychological needs. Individualised hypnobirthing is a holistic approach, incorporating your personal history, your current mindset, and your future aspirations into the birth process. This method recognises that you are not just another statistic, but also an individual with a unique neurocognitive structure. It provides customised tools and techniques that resonate with your unique set of experiences and perceptions. It aims to shape your birthing journey into a positive, empowering experience, no matter your past experiences or present fears.

Turn the page to curate your own individualised brain experience.

Bespoke hypnobirthing

While there are general principles and techniques in hypnobirthing, it is important to recognise that every individual is unique and may resonate with different approaches. Individualised hypnobirthing is about honouring your unique journey and creating an experience that aligns with your needs and desires.

1. Explore different techniques

Experiment with different hypnobirthing techniques and find what works best for you. This could involve trying different visualisations, affirmations, or relaxation exercises to discover what resonates with your mindset and preferences.

2. Customise affirmations

Create your own affirmations that reflect your beliefs and desires for your birth experience. Tailor them to address any specific fears or concerns you may have and focus on empowering and positive statements that resonate with you.

3. Personalise visualisations

Visualisations are a powerful tool in hypnobirthing. Customise your visualisations by envisioning your ideal birth scenario, incorporating specific details that are meaningful to you. Visualise yourself feeling calm, confident, and in control, surrounded by a supportive birthing environment.

4. Adapt breathing techniques

Experiment with different breathing techniques and find the ones that help you achieve a deep state of relaxation. Adjust the pace, rhythm, and duration of the breaths to suit your comfort and preferences. You may also explore combining breathwork with movement or vocalisations, if that feels more natural to you.

5. Incorporate personal touches

Infuse your hypnobirthing practice with personal elements that bring you joy and comfort. This could include playing your favourite music, using essential oils or scents that evoke positive emotions, or surrounding yourself with meaningful objects or symbols.

REMINDER

Trust your instincts, explore different techniques, and adapt them to suit your individuality. By making hypnobirthing your own, you can cultivate a sense of empowerment and peace as you prepare for birth.

BRAIN Key points

Hollywood BS

Drop the false narrative around birth! You've been conditioned to believe birth is something to fear and that your body doesn't know what to do. This is your permission slip to leave the BS behind and move forward with new true intentions and beliefs about your ability to birth.

Purposeful pain

Pain in birth is not your enemy, it's your key messenger, it wants you to surrender, lean in, and trust that it's bringing you and your baby together. Imagine riding those waves. You've got this!

Who are you?

Understanding the real you is going to change the way you birth. Once you've built that new relationship with yourself, you'll start to understand what will and won't work for you during birth, whether that's more privacy or additional support. Knowing the real you is key to feeling good about your experience.

Brain buzzers

Buzz buzz! What better way to tap into the good shit than through brain buzzers? They are your way of connecting through your senses to access those feel-good memories and hormones. Work with these buzzers daily.

Reframing

Reframing your brain is a powerful tool to get rid of the shitty bits and start creating a subconscious that is aligned with your wants and desires for birth. Dig into your brain library and get organising.

Individual hypnobirthing

Hypnobirth with intention! Instead of generic tracks, choose music that resonates. Create your own playlist or find one that gives you the feels. Lean into techniques that feel right for you and know that mindset is everything.

BODY

Connecting with your body

In a world filled with preconceived beauty standards and unrealistic expectations, it's easy to feel pressured by the concrete weight of self-doubt and insecurities.

When you open the door to self-acceptance, you're gaining confidence that's imperative to your birth experience. It's time to shed that concrete and reveal the masterpiece inside of you!

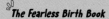

Unveiling your power

When we really connect to our bodies through self-acceptance and love, we can surrender to the beauty and pleasure of birth.

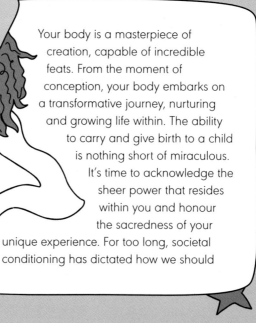

Your body is a masterpiece of creation, capable of incredible feats. From the moment of conception, your body embarks on a transformative journey, nurturing and growing life within. The ability to carry and give birth to a child is nothing short of miraculous. It's time to acknowledge the sheer power that resides within you and honour the sacredness of your unique experience. For too long, societal conditioning has dictated how we should

feel about our bodies. It has often silenced our voices, making us feel powerless and unworthy. You've been led to believe that your period, bodily changes, hairs, stretch marks, and "mum bod" are something to be ashamed of or hidden away. You know what I say? Fuck off! Be gone with this bullshit! It's time to challenge these norms and redefine beauty on your own terms. Celebrate the uniqueness of your body and embrace every aspect that makes you who you are.

Throughout history, you have been sidelined, spoken over, and told what to do. But in this moment, you decide. You are the storyteller, the main character, and the audience, all at once.

You are good enough

Accepting your body can help you feel more confident about birth. The path to self-acceptance starts with you!

It's time to look beyond the superficial and truly see the beauty that lives within you. By cultivating self-awareness and practising self-love, you can start to appreciate the incredible intricacies of your body. From the curves that tell stories of growth and resilience to the scars that signify strength, every part of your body has a tale to tell. The transformative experience of birth can be an important part of a woman's self-acceptance journey.

Intricacies of your body

Birth is a moment that defies description, filled with raw strength, vulnerability, and profound beauty. In this section, we will explore the wonders of your body and sexuality, how this links into birth, and celebrate how you can work with it to create a harmonious body connection.

I've finally found comfort and acceptance within myself and my sexuality. Reflecting on the years lost to self-doubt, shame, and lack of confidence filled me with a sense of urgency to break this generational pattern. Anxiety was my constant companion throughout my 20s, its grip tight on my being, riding me like a wild rodeo, while I spiralled into sporadic and depressing behaviours. I became a master of performance, living out the programming that I mentioned earlier. With fake smiles and an air of confidence on the dance floor, I became the real-life black swan. People would say, "I wish I were as confident as you." Little did they know the constant battle I was fighting within myself, searching desperately for love as if it were a scarce resource. Self-doubt led me

Birth is a moment that defies description, filled with raw strength, vulnerability, and profound beauty.

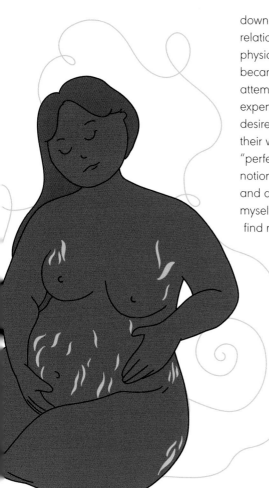

down dark paths, including abusive relationships that took a toll on me physically and emotionally. Sex became a performance, a desperate attempt to please my partners at the expense of my own needs and desires. I thought that by prioritising their wants and desires, I could be the "perfect" girlfriend. It was the classic notion of being a "freak in the sheets and a lady on the streets". I moulded myself into someone else, only to find myself constantly unsatisfied, both emotionally and sexually. Society made me question my own sexuality and body, leaving me feeling inadequate.

The ideals portrayed by Hollywood and porn created a narrow and distorted view of womanhood, limiting my understanding and true worth. But we are so much more than just our bodies.

Your body belongs to you

Let's deep dive into the concept of body autonomy. The truth is, babe, your body belongs to you and only you.

Your body is not just a vessel; it's a force of limitless potential and strength. But you know what? Society has tried to put a lid on that power for far too long. It's tried to dictate what you should know about your body and make choices for you. It's time to rise above those limitations and reclaim your autonomy. Let's explore why this is so important in shaping your experiences and decisions, especially regarding the mind-blowing journey of childbirth.

Understanding body autonomy

Body autonomy means you can decide about your body without anyone else's interference. It's about controlling what happens to your body during pregnancy and birth and ensuring that your choices and boundaries are respected. No one – and I mean no one – has the right to touch your body without your explicit consent. Whether it's a medical professional or anyone else, you have the right to say no and set boundaries. It's essential to remember that your body is yours and yours alone, and you have the legal and moral right to protect it. Your consent cannot be forced or manipulated out of you – it is your choice, babe, and it should always be respected. Advocating for yourself and asserting your body autonomy during pregnancy and birth is crucial. Surround yourself with a supportive birth team who will honour your decisions, listen to your concerns, and respect your boundaries.

Remember, you have the right to make choices that align with your values, beliefs, and desires for your birth experience. So, stand tall, speak up, and assert your body autonomy. You are in control, and no one can take that away. Your body, your choices, your power!

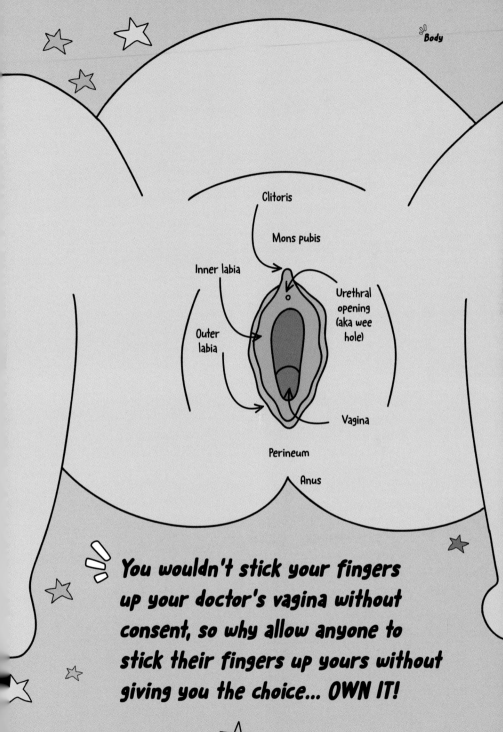

Clitoris

Mons pubis

Inner labia

Outer labia

Urethral opening (aka wee hole)

Vagina

Perineum

Anus

You wouldn't stick your fingers up your doctor's vagina without consent, so why allow anyone to stick their fingers up yours without giving you the choice... OWN IT!

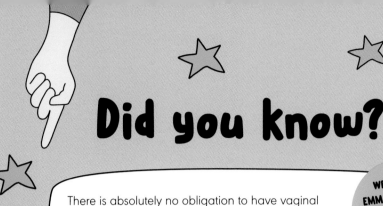

Did you know?

WRITTEN BY
EMMA ASHWORTH
Birth rights
activist and
author

There is absolutely no obligation to have vaginal examinations (VEs) in labour. This includes if you are told that you can't get access to the hospital, or pain relief, without one. You're likely to be told that they need to know whether you're in "active labour" before they'll admit you to hospital. They may say the same about having the midwife stay at home with you at a home birth, before they'll support you getting into the pool or having an epidural or other medical pain relief.

VEs do NOT tell us how much longer our labour will last. Furthermore, you have now been told that you will be denied the care you need unless you agree to a VE, and this means that you are now under duress (meaning you are in a position where you have to comply with their demand to give you a VE if you want to access the hospital/midwife at home). Once you are told that you "have to" have a VE to access the care you need, you are now under duress and therefore you cannot consent to the VE.

You have the right to access maternity care – whether that's at the hospital or at home. And you have the right to pain relief. If a VE accurately told us how far through labour you were, and how long you had to go, it might be a reasonable part of the decision-making process around whether or not it's the right time for you to be in hospital, have a midwife at your home, or have an epidural. But, it doesn't, so it isn't, and you do not have to.

As always, there is nuance here, and it might be that the midwife or doctor is looking for more information than just how open or soft your cervix is. Commuication is key – ask what needs to be known from the VE, what the benefit of that information is, and how it relates to the care you want to access, to make an informed decision.

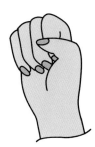

You can say no

- You can choose where to give birth regardless of your pregnancy and/or medical condition.

- You have the right to pain relief during labour if you need it and you cannot be denied this.

- You can say NO to any intervention, medical procedure, blood test, or exam.

- No one should perform any exam or procedure without your informed consent, including a vaginal exam or sweep.

- You have the right to a water birth regardless of your BMI or medical condition.

- No one can force you onto the bed, into a position, or into a procedure, even an emergency Caesarean, without your permission.

Red flags

Some people may try to scare you into changing what you want for your birth. Watch out for coercive language that may undermine your decisions.

Words and phrases to look out for

- I wouldn't do that if I were you
- You want a healthy baby, right?
- If you don't allow us to... then you can't do/have...
- You are being difficult
- I am going to...
- I'm just going to...
- I/we can't allow you...
- You have to...
- Do you want a dead baby?
- It's policy
- You can't...
- We have to do... because you are HIGH RISK
- If you decline...
- What can you do?

Care providers, friends, or family may use certain tactics and words to nudge you into doing something you don't want to do. A lot of these comments may be down to their policies or anxieties. This can then drench you in thoughts of anxiety and worry. Red flags may not come in a rude, aggressive tone... nope, sometimes it can sound kind and helpful.

Change the game

Let's clarify one thing. Your pregnancy and birth journey should be a haven of comfort, empowerment, and choice. Your care providers are there to offer information with zero bias and unwavering support. I'm talking team support vibes! You should NEVER, ever feel cornered, bullied, or coerced. The truth is, we can't always control who we talk to or who we are faced with, and we definitely can't control what people say. However, there are some things we can do for ourselves leading up to and during birth, and also after.

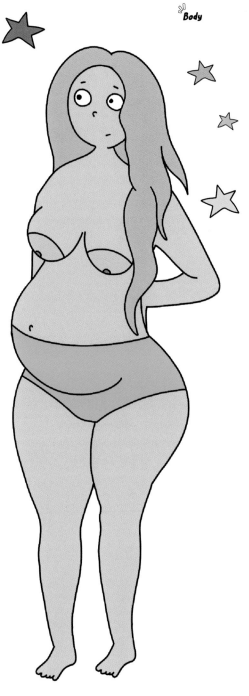

Prep is your secret sauce, babe. Wrap your head around your birth and fill yourself with the knowledge and confidence to navigate conversations and challenges. This is like unlocking a superpower - you'll be walking around with this confidence. You can hear tough stuff, process it, and respond like a birthing ninja. Saying "no", asking for more details, making changes, or being assertive becomes as easy as a deep breath.

If you can, have your birth partner and a doula in your corner. They're your people, your voice, your advocates. When you communicate with your care team, you're not just speaking - you're making sure they hear your rights loud and clear. Don't be afraid to speak up if you ever encounter coercive language, experience an assault, or hear any BS. Don't suffer in silence! Before reporting, make sure to document everything about wrongful care — this includes medical records, personal experiences, dates, times, names of involved personnel, and any correspondence.

The policy is there to guide not to govern your birth experience.

Trimester timeline

Your body will go through some wild changes throughout pregnancy, and while this looks different to everyone, it's good to know what you may expect. Remember, embrace each change with grace and know that you're not alone in these changes.

Tip: Don't have enough room in your bra anymore? You're not alone. Before you run to buy a new bra, try buying a cheap bra extension instead. So smart!

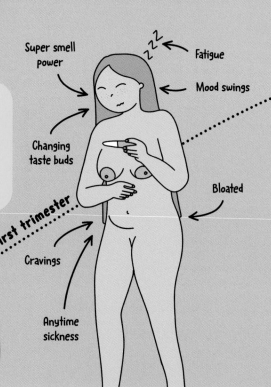

Super smell power

Fatigue

Mood swings

Changing taste buds

Bloated

First trimester

Cravings

Anytime sickness

TO SHAVE OR NOT TO SHAVE? NO NEED TO AT ALL! BUT IF YOU DO, TRY TO ENSURE IT'S DONE IN ADVANCE OF BIRTH TO PREVENT INFECTION RISK AND GROW-BACK ITCHINESS.

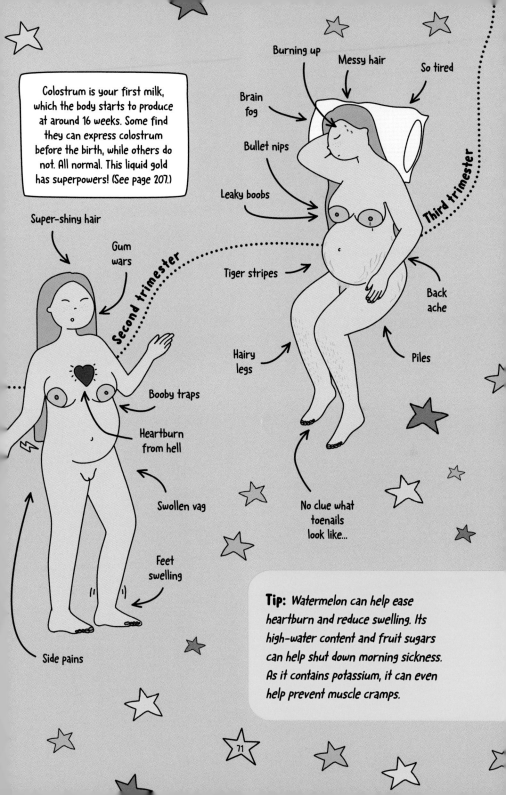

What happens during birth

Let's break birth down in simple terms, because it can get pretty overwhelming.

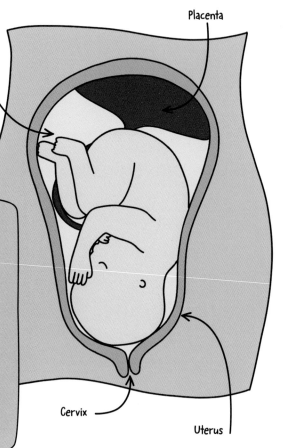

Placenta

Amniotic sac

THE UTERINE WALL IS MADE UP OF THREE LAYERS OF MUSCLE TISSUE.

Getting ready for birth

1. Signals start to occur between baby and body
2. Nerve impulses from the cervix are transmitted to the brain
3. The brain tells the pituitary gland to secrete oxytocin
4. Oxytocin stimulates contractions to move baby and dilate the cervix

Cervix

Uterus

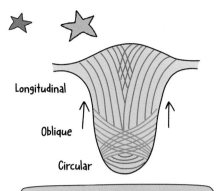

Longitudinal

Oblique

Circular

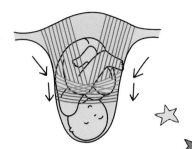

The uterus is made up of longitudinal, circular, and oblique muscles entwined between a connective tissue of blood vessels, elastic fibres, and collagen fibres – stretchy! Each time a contraction starts to rise the vertical (longitude) and rounded (oblique) muscles start to pull up. This draws the horizontal (circular) muscles up, helping to dilate the cervix.

Throughout labour the contractions rise in intensity and become more regular. We can help the uterus by relaxing our bodies as much as possible. Once your baby is ready to be born, which may not yet be at full dilation, you'll notice your contractions change. At this point, your muscles, now pulled up tight, will start pushing baby out and down the birth canal.

Before your baby is born, your cervix will efface (become thinner) and then start to dilate (open) to let the baby through. In subsequent births, effacement and dilation happen together.

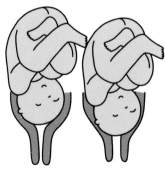

Cervix not effaced. Length of canal 4cm (1½in).

Cervix partly effaced. Length of canal 2cm (¾in).

Cervix fully effaced.

Cervix dilated 3cm (1in).

Cervix dilated 8cm (3in).

You may hear that your cervix will dilate to 10cm (4in), but every cervix is not the same – fully dilated for you could be 8cm (3in) while for others it may be more.

"I trusted my body,
embraced each contraction,
and understood the
importance of protecting
my oxytocin."

Hormones in a nutshell

Endorphins, nature's painkillers, play a vital role in labour. They act as mood boosters, helping you cope with the intensity of contractions. Endorphins block pain signals by binding to the end of your nerve receptors, providing comfort and ease. They also positively impact emotional well-being.

Prolactin prepares your body for breastfeeding and nurtures your maternal instincts. It rises during pregnancy and peaks after birth, stimulating breastmilk production and fostering nurturing behaviours. It deepens the bond with your baby, igniting your innate ability to care for and protect them.

Adrenaline and noradrenaline activate your fight, freeze, or flight response, increasing heart rate and blood pressure, which can lower oxytocin and halt labour if triggered in the early stages. However, they are still vital and provide much-needed energy and alertness when you're gearing up to that final push. As I like to say - they're not your friend until the end!

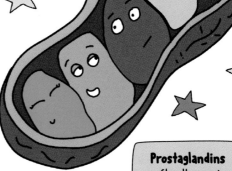

Prostaglandins soften the cervix and stimulate uterine contractions.

Relaxin loosens ligaments and joints, particularly in the pelvis, to accommodate the growing baby. It creates more space for the baby to pass through the birth canal, facilitating a smoother birth. However, be mindful of its effects on other joints and ligaments. Embrace the flexibility but avoid overstretching or straining during pregnancy.

AND THEN THERE'S OXYTOCIN, THE QUEEN HORMONE!

Oxytocin – The queen of birth

This queen is the VIP of hormones. She leads by example and orchestrates your whole labour, birth, and bonding with your baby.

The oxytocin cycle

· The more oxytocin, the better the contraction and the smoother and faster you'll dilate.
· The more oxytocin, the more endorphins.
· More endorphins = less pain and altered state of consciousness - binding to the end of your nerve receptors, blocking pain signals.
· An altered state of consciousness allows us to access the state of mind we need for birth.

Oxytocin is the hormone triggered by the activation of your vagus nerve (part of your parasympathetic nervous system). Oxytocin is the key to survival as she favours reproduction and protects against predators and environmental changes.
It's an extremely important

Is it safe to come out?

What Oxytocin LOVES & HATES

Oxytocin loves
Darkness. Breathing.
Calmness. Laughing.
Love. Bonding. Kissing.
Support. Privacy.
Trust.

Oxytocin hates
Fear. Stress. Bright light.
Being ignored. No support.
Anxiety. Interruptions.
Distractions. Negative
language.

brain compound in building trust and is necessary for developing emotional relationships. Oxytocin counteracts the effects of cortisol, the stress hormone, and less stress means increased pleasure and even pain-free births! Studies show us that it is calming and can have a domino effect on those around you. Without this goddess, labour wouldn't happen, and babies wouldn't be born. Respect this queen and watch how she can influence your birth experience.

Warm and cosy

Imagine a wild sheep, preparing to welcome her lamb into the world. She finds herself a calm, dark, warm, and safe space. Oxytocin loves this feeling, which brings her baby closer and closer to her, BUT THEN, a pesky lion starts to prowl nearby. That sheep will instantly go into danger mode, oxytocin will cease, the body will react and the cervix will go "fuck no". It could even close to keep the lamb inside should the danger be imminent.

Oxytocin is the key hormone that drives your labour. It causes your uterus to contract, which in turn dilates the cervix. We're not passive participants in this; we can actively influence the production of oxytocin and, in turn, potentially influence the progression of labour, how it feels, and the outcome. You can do this by tapping into those brain buzzers, getting that super birth team around you, and creating the perfect birth environment.

Turn to page 138 to find out about creating your ideal environment for birth.

The sex and birth connection

What gets baby in, gets baby out! Understanding this concept is crucial for accessing a euphoric birth experience.

The more comfortable you are with your body and sexuality, the more likely you'll be able to listen and react to what your body needs, which is especially important during labour. Sex can be a big deal when it comes to birth. Oxytocin is the same hormone that peaks during an orgasm and sexual activity. Sex is a word that often triggers different emotions inside of us, but for those comfortable with their sexuality, it can enhance your birth journey. Society has made us feel shame around sex. It has taken away the POWER of our vaginas, and I'm here to reignite that fire and show you just how powerful your yoni really is!

Imagine you and your partner are in the mood for some wild lovin', with oxytocin flowing like a waterfall. Now, imagine taking that steamy session to your garden, and suddenly your nosy neighbours start showing up. Here comes Brian, your self-proclaimed sex expert neighbour, giving pointers on when to "push" and how to "do it right." Talk about a mood killer! I don't think those juices would be flowing for very long. Well, guess what – the same goes for birth. That feeling of embarrassment and lack of privacy may interfere with oxytocin, which then may interfere with labour, leading to interventions. Your birth space is your space and you should feel comfortable with those around you. When you're comfortable and have that trust, oxytocin flows freely, making your birth journey so much smoother and more enjoyable. It's all about privacy and good vibes.

The power of orgasms

Orgasms have been found to have a remarkable effect on the body's health. Boom! Studies have shown that orgasms can reduce and even eliminate pain during contractions and birth. When you experience an orgasm, your body releases a flood of oxytocin. This surge can have an incredible pain-relieving effect, helping you navigate the intensity of childbirth with more ease and comfort. French psychologist Thierry Postel conducted a study exploring the effects of sexual stimulation on pain during labour. The study found that those who engaged in clitoral stimulation during contractions experienced a significant reduction in pain intensity. Orgasms also trigger the release of endorphins, the body's natural painkillers, providing a natural and blissful way to manage discomfort. Another study published in the journal "Sexual and Relationship Therapy" tested sexual stimulation as a pain relief method during childbirth.

The findings revealed that women who engaged in sexual activity such as masturbation experienced reduced pain levels and a greater sense of control during labour. If you want to

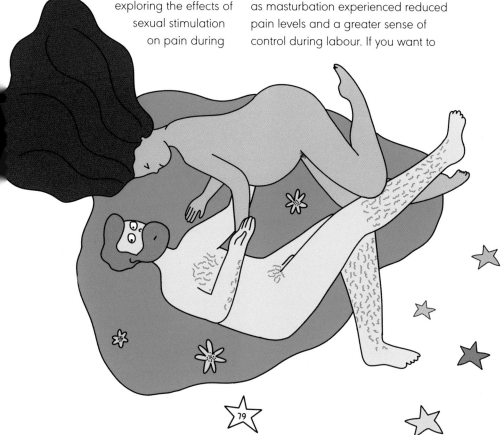

"My labour was an orgasmic act of love. It was unique and powerful. I had a feeling of joy and pleasure. I controlled my mind, surrendering my body while giving birth."

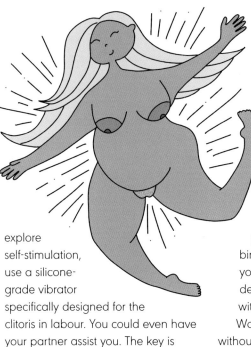

not work for another. The focus here is on embracing the potential benefits that touch can offer during childbirth. By tapping into the power of pleasure, you can enhance the release of oxytocin, reduce pain, and create a more positive and empowering birth experience. So, don't be afraid to explore the possibility of pleasure during birth if it resonates with you. Trust your body's wisdom, listen to your desires, and communicate openly with your birth team.

explore self-stimulation, use a silicone-grade vibrator specifically designed for the clitoris in labour. You could even have your partner assist you. The key is communicating your desires and comfort levels with your birth team to ensure a supportive and respectful environment.

Want to experience euphoria without the orgasm? Creating a completely undisturbed birth experience with only LOVE and SUPPORT and SURRENDER can lead to orgasmic experiences without flicking the bean! Think tantric. Breathwork, energy, and pure power!

At the hospital

How do you do this in a hospital environment? Ask for some privacy, or use the bathroom. Remember, you can choose who's in the room at any point and what you do with your body is for you to decide!

Every birth experience is unique, and what works for one person may

OUTER STIMULATION ONLY, BABES!

 Sexual activity can reduce pain levels and improve your sense of control.

Training for birth

You can train your body in smart ways to gain strength and control for the moment of birth.

The alignment and condition of our bodies play a significant role in creating an optimal birthing experience. By implementing a few simple exercises and practices into your daily routine, you can train your body for the transformative journey ahead.

Visit a chiropractor and osteopath
Seeing a pregnancy chiropractor and osteopath can help to align your pelvis so that your baby can descend more easily down the birth canal. They can also help with breech babies,

Daily walking
Walking 2–5km (1–3 miles) per day allows your body to balance naturally. Keep your head held high, move at your own pace, and breathe in some fresh air.

Get on the pregnancy yoga
Pregnancy yoga can help to balance the body and prepare you for a more effortless birthing experience. Try finding a local class or videos online at home. BUT if you're hypermobile, maybe less stretching and more strengthening.

Squatting for the win
Stick to parallel squats (where the bum doesn't go lower than the pelvis and knees don't go out further than the foot). Avoid deep squats until you're in established labour.

Forward leaning inversion
Doing this exercise daily may aid in good foetal positioning by untwisting and stretching ligaments connected to the lower uterus and cervix. Ensure you follow the Spinning Babies® guidelines (see page 217).

Kneel on the edge of a couch Let your head hang freely with chin inwards.

Rest on your forearms. Take three breaths. Try this for 30 seconds a day.

REMINDER

Each body is unique, and it's essential to listen to your body's signals and adjust your exercises and practices accordingly. Always check with your care provider before consuming anything for labour and birth, especially if you have gestational diabetes.

Raspberry leaf tea

Raspberry leaf is most commonly ingested as a tea or in tablet form. Its purpose is to help strengthen and tone the uterus for birth and prevent haemorrhage. The leaves are rich in antioxidants and nutrients such as calcium, iron, and potassium, as well as containing vitamins A, C, and E. Studies have shown a shorter second stage of labour for women consuming raspberry leaf tea from 32 weeks' gestation. For those with diabetes, consumption might lower glucose levels, lowering insulin requirements. The adverse effects potentially outweigh

the benefits, so always check with your midwife whether this herbal birth booster is for you.

Superfruit of birth

Studies show women who ate six dates a day for the four weeks leading up to their due date were: 74% more dilated, 21% more likely to go into labour spontaneously, 28% less likely to use artificial oxytocin to induce labour and had a 77% shorter first stage of labour. Eat six small dates from 36 weeks to soak in these benefits. Hate the taste? Try sticking them in a smoothie! Other juicy benefits: reduces the chance of postpartum haemorrhage; stimulates uterine contractions; regulates blood pressure; oxytocin-like effect.

Party through labour

⭐ Music, rhythm, and movement have special powers when it comes to birth. They lift your spirits and also work magic on your body and mind.

The dance of birth

Dancing during birth is like having a secret weapon in your birth toolkit. The best part is, you don't need to be a pro dancer by any means. Babe, just get that music going and do YOU. The beauty of dancing during labour is that it's not just about having a good time (although that's an amazing bonus). It's also about how movement can work wonders during the birthing process. When you dance, you work with gravity to ease the intensity of contractions and help your baby find the best position for their grand entrance. Here's the

- **Benefits**
- Boosts oxytocin
- Encourages upright positioning and movement
- Speeds up dilation
- May shorten the duration of labour

- Helps change attitude and emotional state
- Decreases likelihood of operative birth
- Less likely to have an epidural, with overall lower pain intensity

best part: studies have shown that dancing during the first stage of labour can actually decrease the need for additional pain relief and make your birthing experience more satisfying. Game-changer!

What about when things start to get intense?

It's like going from a fun party to a slow and sensual dance. During the early stages of labour, you can move and groove to your heart's content. But as things get deeper and more intense, you may find yourself wanting to slow down and sway with your baby in a gentle, rhythmic motion. One way to take advantage of movement during labour is belly dancing. It's not just for Shakira – it's for all the birthing queens out there. Belly dancing involves graceful hip sways and gentle undulations, mimicking the natural flow of birth. It's a beautiful way to open up your pelvis and create space for your baby to descend. So, when the time comes, put on your favourite tunes, turn up the volume, and let the dance party begin. Dance your way through those contractions, and when things get deeper, switch to that slow dance mode. Remember, this is your birthing journey, and you've got the moves to make it extraordinary!

Tips for energising
· Natural energy drinks
· Bananas
· Dates
· Breakfast bars
· Wholegrain snacks
· Water
· HACK: Make ice cubes out of your favourite fruit juice or smoothie and suck on them.

Check out some hip-opening birth positions on page 90.

The magic of music

From the moment the first note hits your ears, music sets the stage for an extraordinary experience. But it's not just about creating ambiance; music has a direct line to your brain, and it's one of your most important brain buzzers. When you listen to music that resonates with you, your brain lights up. It triggers a beautiful symphony of positive memories and emotions, releasing feel-good hormones and that precious oxytocin. Through labour, the love hormone takes centre stage, helping you connect with your baby and easing your way.

Listening to music of your choice during labour decreases postpartum anxiety and pain, and increases childbirth satisfaction. Use earphones throughout your journey to the birth centre/hospital, along with an eye-mask for optimal oxytocin levels.

What's your frequency?

396 Hz: This frequency is known and shown to change your mood from shitty to a shitload of happy.
417 Hz: This frequency is AMAZING for anxiety and useful for healing trauma. Used all over the world to treat stress.
528 Hz: This frequency is the one which nature vibrates at. It's also used to treat cancers. WOAH! No joke – it's believed to repair damaged DNA.
963 Hz: This frequency is shown to help you connect with your inner child and surrender. This is GAME-CHANGING for labour and oxytocin production.

When it comes to creating your playlist, remember to keep it unique and personal. This is your birthing soundtrack, and it should resonate with your heart and soul. Create two playlists – one for when the party's just getting started, and another for the deeper stages of labour when you want to slow down and savour the magical moments. Fill your playlists with songs that speak to you, that hold special memories, or that simply make you feel good. This is your chance to curate a musical masterpiece that will accompany you every step of the way.

"I had chosen calm and
emotional songs that really
meant something to me and
even remember being flooded
with emotions and having a
good cry about tranistioning
into motherhood."

KICO: Knees in calves out

KICO (knees in, calves out! I've got the pelivc tricks to help your bits. Let's break it down...

Your pelvis is like a masterful puzzle, made up of bones, joints, and ligaments. During birth, it transforms into a magical passageway, guiding your little one into the world. The pelvis isn't a rigid structure, it can shift and move to create more space for your baby's descent. The hormone relaxin, released during pregnancy, further enhances the flexibility of the pelvis, making it more pliable and adaptive.

Think about the dance you'll be having during that labour party... Dancing and moving is the BEST way to change the shape of your pelvis and give your baby all they need for movement. Listen to those instincts and find positions that work well. The beautiful thing about all of this is that as baby descends down the pelvis and birth canal, their skull moves and moulds. Yes! Your baby's head is like a master of flexibility, so it's defo not like "SHITTING OUT A WATERMELON" and more like pushing out a nice ripe avocado. Mouldable and scrumptious!

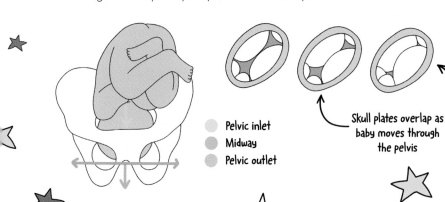

Pelvic inlet
Midway
Pelvic outlet

Skull plates overlap as baby moves through the pelvis

"I gave birth in KICO position on all fours. I breathed her out, and it was so pleasant! I felt confident in myself and my body in every movement."

Positions to open the pelvic inlet

The pelvic inlet is the top of the pelvis. Positions to open the pelvic inlet may help during the start of labour. It can help baby to drop down into the midway point of the pelvis.

Squatting

This position widens the pelvic outlet and allows gravity to assist the baby's descent. It's a powerful way to open the pelvic inlet and facilitate the birthing process.

Birthing ball

Sitting and gently rocking on a birthing ball can open the pelvic inlet and provide comfort during labour.

Side-lying

Lying on your side with one leg raised can help open the pelvic inlet and promote optimal positioning for the baby.

Positions to help open up the mid-portion of the pelvis

The midway point of the pelvis is when baby is fully engaged and on their way down the pelvis. Asymmetrical movements can help create space and movement in the pelvis helping to bring baby down.

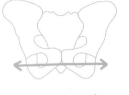

Lunges

Performing lunges, either supported or unsupported, can help open the pelvic inlet and encourage the baby's head to engage in the pelvis.

Hands and knees

Being on all fours, with hands and knees on the ground, allows for a gentle rocking motion of the pelvis. This position helps in maintaining pelvic mobility and can be particularly helpful in cases of a posterior baby position.

Side walking up stairs

This engages the pelvis muscles and ligaments, promoting flexibility and mobility. It also balances the pelvis, beneficial for babies in asymmetrical positions.

Opening the pelvic outlet using KICO

The pelvic outlet is the bottom of the pelvis where baby will descend. You can create more space in the pelvic outlet by using KICO (knees in calves out) or parallel. This can be used when baby is low down or ready to be born.

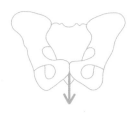

Bring your knees closer together while keeping your calves wider apart. This doesn't have to be dramatic! Even bringing them parallel with each other or turning your feet slightly inwards can do the trick! This mighty movement opens up the pelvic outlet, creating a clear path for your baby's grand entrance. And don't forget the magical movement of the sacrum too! Keeping the sacrum free to move outward is crucial for the baby's descent.

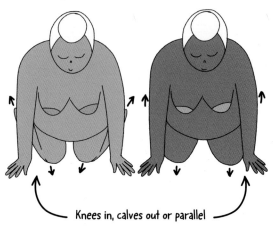

Knees in, calves out or parallel

Tip: *Avoid lying on your lower back in a semi-supine position as this can inhibit the sacrum from its natural movement, increasing interventions.*

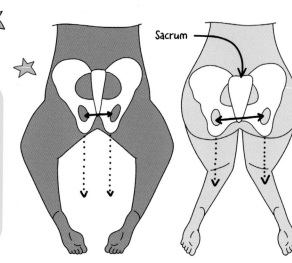

Sacrum

KICO positions and where to use them

Standing up

On hands and knees

Side-lying

On the bed

When to use KICO
- The second stage
- Could help a back-to-back baby
- Later stages of labour
- Birthing your baby
- Not at all if it doesn't feel right

Squatting

REMINDER

Labour is not linear. When deciding on positions during labour and birth it's imperative to listen to your body. Your baby and body will know what to do, when, and how to feel comfortable. Intuition always trumps textbooks. So if you feel called to lie down - DO IT!

In the pool

Floppy face, floppy fanny

Your jaw and pelvic floor are bezzie mates. Tense jaw? Tense pelvic floor. So remember that where the jaw goes, the pelvic floor will follow!

Floppy face, floppy fanny is the mantra that gets repeated in almost every single birth story sent to me. There are so many connections between the jaw and the pelvic floor. If you're able to remember this mantra during birth, it can help to ease tension, allow more elasticity, increase oxytocin and blood flow, and allow your perineum to stretch for your baby.

Soft face
=
soft vagina

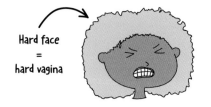

Hard face
=
hard vagina

You can even practise during sex...

If you want to, you can even use FFFF to make your orgasms more intense! When you allow your face to relax, EVERYTHING becomes easier. The pelvic floor is a group of muscles and other tissues that act as a hammock across the pelvis. It holds important organs such as the uterus, bladder, and bowel in place so they can work properly. If we PULL the hammock tight, the pelvic floor muscles lift the internal organs of the pelvis and tighten the openings of the vagina, anus, and urethra, meaning we restrict space and prevent our uterus muscles from working efficiently. If we RELAX our pelvic floor, we allow for space, movement, and the easing of our uterus to contract, allowing for smoother dilation. And when it comes to pushing, it's all about focusing on that same technique. This is how you allow your baby to make their way down and out with ease and elasticity.

The technique

Alright, goddesses of birth, are you ready for a cheeky but transformative technique? Let's dive into the wonderfully whimsical world of the "floppy face, floppy fanny" technique! And trust me, as quirky as it sounds, there's some real magic behind this one.

1. Achieving the floppy face: *Resting bitch face:* Yep, that same look you give when someone tells you they're "just not into chocolate" (I mean, who are these people?). It's about allowing your face muscles to completely relax.

Soft mouth: Drop that jaw slightly, let your lips part, and allow your tongue to sit softly against the roof of your mouth. This isn't about looking like a magazine cover, it's about feeling relaxed and real.

2. Now, down to the fanny: Once your face is all chill, bring your awareness down to your pelvic region. Feel that connection? As the face goes floppy, envision your pelvic muscles also letting go, creating a gentle, welcoming space for your baby.

3. Breath connection: Incorporate mindful, slow breaths. As you breathe in, picture the oxygen swirling through your body, bringing calmness. As you exhale, let go of any remaining tension in both your face and your pelvis.

4. Practice makes perfect: While waiting for a coffee or sitting in traffic, practise the technique. If you make it a habit, it will be easier to summon that relaxation when the real deal happens. Try using this technique when you're about to orgasm or while you're trying for that stubborn poo! Watch the difference.

Riding the wave

Breathwork is an underdog. Forgotten but always coming out on top, with major benefits for your physical and mental well-being. Focus on breathing and find yourself riding the wave like a pro!

Deep and rhythmic breathing increases oxygen intake and triggers the release of endorphins, those SAS bad boys! They're the ones who help manage pain and create a positive emotional state, making you feel more empowered and in control. They're also the boss when it comes to releasing shit that no longer serves you. Think of deep breathing as your personal relaxation guru. Feeling those contractions? With each breath, you'll find them becoming a rhythm rather than a hurdle. With every consistent, deep inhale and exhale, you're sending love letters filled with oxygen to both you and your little one. It ensures your energy tank stays full and your baby gets the VIP treatment.

Envisioning contractions as waves can transform your labour. By riding the wave, you become not just an observer but a surfer, rising to meet each wave with the grace, power, and determination of a goddess. Remember, each wave brings your baby closer.

Contractions feel different to everyone and can change depending on baby's position; however, most rise in intensity to a peak and then drop. Author Milli Hill shares some great facts on contractions stating that in an average 8-hour first stage, your time having contractions is only 23%. The other 77% is pain-free. Most find the peak of the contraction really hard work, which equates to only 7.7% of labour time being really painful. The peak only lasts 10–20 seconds.

Deep breathing during labour

1. Calm and focus Conscious and controlled breathing helps you stay centred and focused. By directing attention to your breath, you can create a sense of calm amidst the intensity of labour. This focused breathing enables you to let go of fear and anxiety, promoting a more serene and empowered mindset.

2. Release and surrender As labour progresses, deep breathing encourages the release of tension and stress. Each exhale can become a symbolic act of surrender, allowing you to trust your body's innate ability to give birth. This release fosters a feeling of openness and receptivity, making way for the baby's arrival.

3. Connection and empowerment Breathing during birth is a tool for connection with the baby and birth partner. It's a shared experience that helps you and your support team feel united and deeply connected. It empowers everyone involved and strengthens your emotional bond.

The peak usually lasts only 10–20 seconds. You can do this!

And breathe...

HOW TO

Initiate with awareness:
As you sense the beginning of a contraction, focus on your breath. Breathe in deeply through your nose, allowing your belly to rise.

Visualise the wave:
Imagine your contraction as a wave. As the contraction builds, visualise the wave rising. Inhale deeply and exhale slowly as the wave begins to rise. Focus on that breath!

Reach the peak:
As the contraction reaches its peak, slowly exhale through soft lips, imagining the top of the wave. Let this exhale be longer than your inhale. Use "horse lips" if you find this bit hard – let your lips vibrate like a horse's!

Surrender to the wave:
After the peak of the contraction, take another deep breath in, envisioning the wave fading. As you exhale, visualise the water drawing back, leaving you in a peaceful calm.

If you need to shout, swear, or be loud, try turning it into low vibrational tones.

REMINDER

Contractions are not the enemy. Once you understand what they are and what is happening inside your body, you'll instantly see and feel things differently!

Jaw, joints, and jazz hands for the peak!

A focus on your jaw, your joints, and your best jazz hands can help manage the peak of your contractions. Here is a step-by-step guide to mastering your unique dilation journey.

Just like giving your favourite plant space to grow, this breathing technique gives your uterus the room it needs. By melting away tension, it allows those powerful muscles to pull up, creating the optimal environment for dilation. Think of it as making your uterus comfy for the big moment!

Wave rider

Those peak moments during contractions can feel intense. But guess what? Focusing on your breath for 10–20 seconds can be q game-changer. It's like catching a wave just right – it distracts the mind and even releases our body's natural feel-good vibes, endorphins!

Chit-chat with baby

The deep connection between you and your baby is undeniable. Keeping your brain calm with this breathing pattern ensures that the communication lines stay open. It's like having a heart-to-heart in the midst of a bustling café – the two of you remain in your cosy bubble, undisturbed. With a calm mind and focused breathing, there's no interruption in transmission. Your body and your baby continue their beautiful conversation, ensuring everything's on track and in harmony.

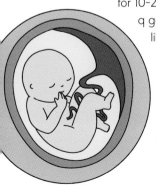

HOW TO

Catch the wave As you sense a contraction's peak approaching, it's showtime. Begin by inhaling slowly, counting up to three. Picture each count as a step up on a gentle incline.

Release the jaw On your exhale, focus on letting your jaw hang loose. It's surprising how much tension we hold here! Imagine your jaw muscles melting like soft wax, releasing any strain. Floppy face, floppy fanny!

Joints - let them flow Pay special attention to your shoulders, allowing them to drop and relax. Envision any tightness flowing away, like water off a duck's back.

Jazz hands finale As you continue to exhale, let your hands drop and fingers wiggle. When we move intentionally we are activating our somatic nervous system. This can divert our attention from the stressor and redirect it towards the movement, offering respite. Think of it as your hands dancing to the music of your breath.

ALTERNATE
"Jaw, joints, and juice"

If you're holding onto a birth comb (a wonderful tactile tool!), follow the same steps as above for the jaw and joints. When you get to the hands, instead of the gentle wiggle, imagine you're holding a ripe fruit, and gently squeeze the comb as if you're juicing it. Feel the gentle pressure and visualise the juice flowing, representing your strength and connection to the birthing process. Remember, the essence of this technique is all about synchronising your breath with body relaxation. So, as you ride each wave, let the "jaw, joints, and jazz hands" (or "juice") method guide you through a harmonious, empowering performance. Here's to your birthing encore!

Breathing baby out

Forget purple pushing and push with purpose! Learn a safer and better way to birth your baby into the world.

Cast your mind back a century. Until the 1920s, the idea of instructing birthing women to "push" wasn't even in the picture. Even if someone was unconscious or in a coma, the magic of the Ferguson reflex, would still bring the baby into the world. Enter the 1920s, and the glamour of Hollywood. Suddenly, forced, or purple, pushing was the "it" thing, framed as the fast-pass ticket to a safe delivery. Half a century later, it dawned on the medical world that holding one's breath and pushing like you're trying to burst a balloon might not be the best way. It leads to declines in oxygen levels, drops in foetal heartbeats, and increased interventions.

In 2016, a UK hospital, embracing the wisdom of ancient birthing practices, launched the Stop Traumatic OASI Morbidity Project (STOMP). It shuns forced pushing, promotes upright births, allows the baby to emerge at its own pace, and uses breathing techniques. And what did they find? A dip in perineal tearing and other vaginal trauma. In fact, the study shed light on how valuable the second stage of labour is for the baby – it stimulates their respiratory and digestive systems and blesses them with beneficial bacteria. The success of the STOMP approach was so resounding that it made its way to the pages of journals, and there's buzz about this model becoming standard in hospitals across the UK. However, the Hollywood-style birth still lingers in many birthing rooms worldwide. It's time to tune back into our bodies and remember that when it comes to birth, nature knows best.

IF YOU REALLY NEED TO PUSH, KEEP YOUR MOUTH OPEN AND USE LOW VIBRATIONAL NOISE.

Let's look at the facts of FORCED PUSHING

- **Decreased oxygen supply** When you hold your breath during intense pushing, the amount of oxygen you inhale is reduced. This means less oxygen is available for transfer to your baby through the placenta, potentially leading to lowered foetal oxygen levels. This can cause your baby's heart rate to drop, which could necessitate emergency interventions.

- **Increased maternal fatigue** Forced pushing is physically and mentally exhausting. The strain can quickly lead to fatigue, which can prolong the birth process.

- **Increased risk of perineal trauma** The intense, forceful pushing associated with this method puts extra pressure on the perineum (the area between the vagina and anus), increasing the risk of tears or the need for an episiotomy (a surgical cut to widen the vaginal opening).

- **Potential impact on pelvic floor muscles** Forceful pushing can strain the pelvic floor muscles, leading to issues such as urinary incontinence or pelvic organ prolapse post-birth.

- **Stress for baby** Decreased oxygen can cause the baby stress, potentially leading to various health issues, such as low Apgar scores or the need for resuscitation at birth.

- **Potential for birth interventions** With the increased risk for foetal distress, there may be a higher likelihood of interventions like Caesarean section or instrumental birth.

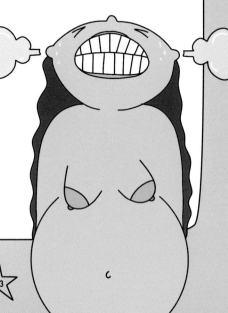

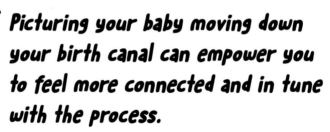

Picturing your baby moving down your birth canal can empower you to feel more connected and in tune with the process.

Breathing baby out

So how the fuck do you "breath your baby out"? There's so much mystique surrounding this phrase! But, babe, it's so much more than just exhaling and waiting for magic to happen. It's not a whimsical blow on a birthday candle with hopes of a tiny human popping out. Yes, the body has its remarkable ways (hello, Ferguson reflex!), but our focus here is on mastering a profound technique.

Diaphragmatic breathing One of the foundational techniques of breathing baby out involves using the diaphragm – the muscle beneath the lungs – to facilitate deeper, more effective breaths. When you breathe deeply into your belly rather than shallow breaths in your chest, you can better channel the force of your diaphragm and abdomen. This kind of breathing maximises oxygen flow to both the mother and baby and encourages the natural downward movement of the baby.

Floppy face, floppy fanny – soft mouth

Keeping the mouth soft and relaxed is crucial. If you do not manage anything else, manage this! A tense jaw mirrors tension in the pelvic area. By ensuring the mouth remains soft and relaxed, possibly even open, this can indirectly help to promote relaxation in the pelvic muscles, allowing the baby to descend more easily.

Combination of breathing and gentle pushing For some, a combination of deep breathing and gentle pushing feels most natural. This can mean taking a deep breath and then using a slight push as you exhale, ensuring you aren't holding your breath but are instead working with your body's breath and rhythm.

Vocalisation Many find power in vocalising during birth. Deep, guttural sounds can be incredibly effective in assisting the descent of your baby. This might be a powerful exhale of noise, a moo, or even roaring, reminiscent of a lion. These sounds are often instinctual and can release tension, help open the throat, and provide a sense of power.

Trusting spontaneous pushing The Ferguson reflex happens when your baby is ready to be born, where the uterus will spontaneously push the baby out without conscious effort. When you are undisturbed and deeply relaxed, you might experience this reflex.

Visualisation Picturing your baby moving down your birth canal can empower you to feel more connected and in tune with the process.

REMINDER

While the technique of "breathing the baby out" offers an alternative method, it's essential for you to find what feels right for your body and to be guided by YOUR instincts and sensations during birth.

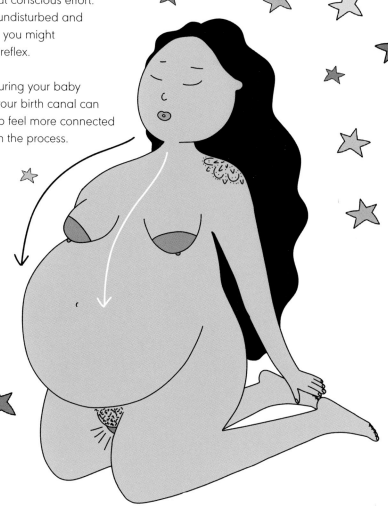

BODY
Key points

Oxytocin and sex

Oxytocin is the queen of birth so respect her wishes to feel comfortable and happy. Don't panic if you don't always feel like this. Oxytocin won't leave you in the midst of labour, she'll always be around, but the more nurturing she gets, the more she'll show up!
Oxytocin is the key hormone during sex and orgasms, so don't be afraid to bring some lovin' into the birth room.

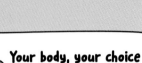

Your body, your choice

If you need a reminder, here it is! Your body is yours; what happens to it is up to you. No one should be doing anything without consent and you should feel comfortable with what's happening. Don't be afraid to speak up!

The body basics

Your gorgeous uterus, with its three muscle layers and the safe home of your baby, will start working some magic. With each contraction, it will pull those muscles up, dilating the cervix and moving your baby down. Remember, oxytocin and endorphins are working together beautifully at this point to create the perfect surge each time.

FFFF and riding the wave

Floppy face, floppy fanny goes hand-in-hand with those big waves. Initiating that relaxed jaw will leave your pelvic floor feeling ahhh and your contractions feeling more manageable. Don't forget the peak FFFF for ultimate dilation.

KICO and positions

Finding positions that feel good is KEY, but knowing what works well in each stage of birth can be really helpful. Breaking the mould of "legs wide open" and instead looking at KICO can help to make space for your babe to be born.

Party through labour

Your labour is a celebration and a time to tune into your vibe. Is it giving dance party or slow and steady vibes? Your labour can look however you want it to look, depending on how you feel. If you're being called to move those hips, sway, and have fun. Not that kind of party? Chill out with slow, intuitive moves that breed focus and calm.

Breathe baby out

We're not talking about blowing out a candle but more intentional breaths, directing that energy downwards and using low vibrational tones if needed. Roar like a lion, be one with your body, and keep that mouth open and soft!

BIRTH

Owning your birth experience

This is YOUR birth, YOUR choice. It's time to ignite that inner Khaleesi. You will walk into the flames of your own incredible power, and walk out like a goddamn queen of your birth!

You have the tools and you have the techniques. All you need now is the lowdown and facts so that YOU can take control and make informed decisions, no matter what path birth takes you down.

Your unique experience

Your unique experience is made by pulling together your wants and desires. It's a pathway that feels aligned with you yet is flexible enough to boss the hell out of any challenge in your way!

Your birth is one of the biggest, most life-changing transformations you'll ever go through. What happens now will shape you, your baby and your future. You will take your vision and translate it into the Naked Doula visual birth plan. This approach holds immense power, because our minds are wired to respond to visuals.

Think of it as gearing up for an epic adventure. You wouldn't set off without a map, supplies, and a clear sense of direction, as well as the know-how to deal with any challenges. Birth is no different!

Being prepared means arming yourself with knowledge, tools, and strategies to navigate this experience. This doesn't mean controlling every detail. From understanding the stages of labour to having relaxation techniques at your fingertips, being prepared empowers you to embrace your birth journey with open arms.

So, gather your tools and step onto this path, fully equipped and ready to conquer whatever comes your way. Some might argue that planning too much takes away from the spontaneity and magic of birth, but here's the truth: preparation is not the same as rigidity. Planning doesn't mean you're scripting every moment of your birth like a Hollywood blockbuster. It's about creating a flexible framework that empowers you to make informed decisions as things unfold. Over-planning can lead to disappointment if things don't go exactly as envisioned, but being prepared means you're adaptable, informed, and resilient.

I know the unpredictability of birth all too well! Being a doula and supporting births in person and online, all over the world, it's clear that no two births are ever the same. This is why I truly believe that the generic standard of care just isn't made to be personal to you, your mind, your body, your beliefs, or your needs. I am extremely passionate about every woman feeling powerful about their choices and happy with their decisions. No one knows your mind and body better than you, which is why it's imperative you're prepared and having open and honest conversations with your care providers.

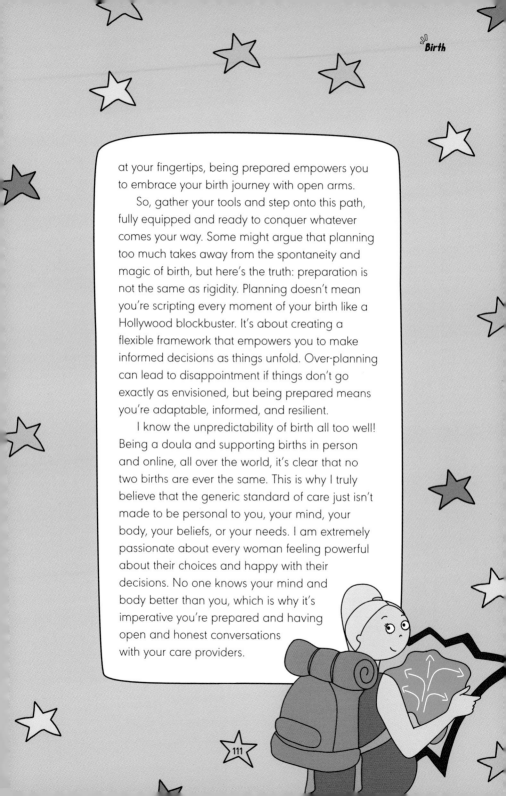

My story

My most recent birth, to George, was unpredictable. This kid did not want to come out! I'd done all the prep and worked on my brain library (see page 38). See, Charlie, my first, was born via elective C-section after a discovery of breech and with no care providers competent enough to assist a vaginal breech birth. I really do think his positioning and the outcome was down to my mum dying of cancer at the 26-week mark of my pregnancy. And yes, it was pretty fucking traumatic. Nethertheless, I found the strength to create and advocate for a stunning, euphoric Caesarean birth experience. Dimmed lights, music, and pure bliss. Extremely spiritual but filled with grief and heartache from losing my own mother.

This time around, with George, I believed I would give birth vaginally, the way I'd longed for and had supported so many others to achieve. But it wasn't in the stars for me. Forty-two weeks crept up and finally my waters started to trickle. Contractions came a few days later and got pretty intense, pretty fast. But then I saw meconium. The baby had pooped inside me. I'd ensured communication was clear throughout my pregnancy, I'd discussed all options, and covered all bases in my plan, including a repeat C-section and emergencies. I had a supportive team including a doula. I was feeling confident and ready to listen to my body. My following was watching with anticipation.

MY COMPLICATIONS IN BIRTH ARE NOT COMMON, BUT I BELIEVE I WAS GIVEN THEM SO THAT I COULD SHARE MY WISDOM WITH THE WORLD.

Now, poop doesn't always mean an emergency, especially so late on in pregnancy, but not knowing whether it was fresh or not, I decided to head in. The hospital policy was against me, being over 42 weeks, broken waters, and now this. But I knew my rights and advocated for a beautiful room in the midwife-led unit.

I had very little intermittent monitoring, used the pool and the shower, and had a serious oxytocin party! I didn't want any pain relief and really felt I didn't need it; the pure joy from riding the strong waves was enough. But after 24 hours, something didn't feel right. Lumps on my cervix were causing issues, the contractions were strong AF, and things weren't making sense. So George was delivered by my own hands via Caesarean in the very same room I birthed Charlie. Every single decision, choice, and outcome was led by me. My intuition didn't do me wrong: had I carried on, it may have been very different.

I believed I would give birth vaginally, the way I longed for and supported so many others to achieve.

How to be truly informed

Here's how to create the perfect visual plan that will support your decisions while being beautifully flexible.

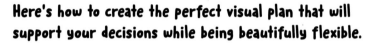

Making informed decisions

Using **BRAIN** as a way to make informed decisions is a way to keep control over what's happening with your birth, body, and baby. You can use this for ANYTHING and EVERYTHING, babes, so listen up!

B.R.A.I.N. =

- What are the **BENEFITS** of accepting or declining?
- What are the **RISKS** of accepting this intervention or decision vs declining?
- What are the **ALTERNATIVES**?
- What does your **INTUITION** say?
- What if you do **NOTHING**, you wait, an hour, a day, a week.
- What does this look and feel like?

Crafting your birth vision is like weaving together your hopes and dreams for the transformative journey of childbirth. Now, imagine taking that beautiful tapestry of intentions and translating it into a visual birth plan. When you create a visual birth plan, whether it's through images, symbols, or even a collage, you're fueling your confidence and deepening your connection to the birthing process. Sharing your visual birth plan with your support team can offer them a window into your heart's desires.

Crafting your visual birth plan is one of the most fun parts of preparing for labour. Not only do you get to use visuals to explain your needs and desires, but you also learn along the way. It helps you to question every outcome and scenario and create guidelines for your experience that align with you, no matter what

How to make decisions for YOU

Each person deserves individualised care. Making decisions based on a set of "generic guidelines" isn't a fair way to weigh up what is right for you and your baby. We are all unique. We all have different circumstances, feelings, and experiences. Therefore, YOU have to take responsibility for your care and actions to ensure you are well-informed and able to make the best decisions for you and your baby.

Facts: Things known or proved to be true.	VS	**Myths:** Misconceptions, false beliefs or ideas.
Knowledge: Understanding your body and birth.	VS	**Unknown:** Going in without a clue.
Trust: Trusting yourself, your body, and your baby.	VS	**Distrust:** Trusting others without getting info or options.
Evidence: Having up-to-date, solid evidence.	VS	**Bias:** No evidence, or low-quality opinions.
Individual: Personal circumstances and history.	VS	**Generic:** One set of rules/ guidelines for all.

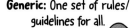

happens. Now, to the juicy part. This piece of labour artwork isn't just for the pretty colours. It's going to take you through each stage of labour and every possible outcome. This way, you can choose how you want this to look, should any of these circumstances occur during labour. Without a plan, you could find yourself lacking control, unsure how to navigate surprises and unexpected changes. So delve in and start creating yours now.

Where and who?

A huge part of your birth plan involves WHERE you choose to give birth and WHO you want to be there.

Homebirth

When you mention homebirth, people might say, "wow, you're brave". But with the medical environment being linked to worse outcomes and the possibility of increased intervention, it's no wonder people are looking to give birth in a place of comfort and familiarity. Anyone can have a home birth regardless of the size, design, or current decor of your home! HOWEVER, home birth is not for everyone, especially if you don't feel safe and happy there.

SAY WHAT?
YOU ARE ENTITLED TO A HOME BIRTH NO MATTER YOUR AGE, SIZE, OR SITUATION!

Pros
· Increased feeling of control
· Influence your environment easily
· Increased sense of satisfaction
· Lower rates of Caesareans
· Lower rates of needing intervention
· Reduced rates of pain relief being needed
· Lower rates of infection

Cons
· No immediate access to an epidural or opioids
· Might make some women feel uncomfortable
· Would have to transfer in case of emergency

REMINDER
Each birth is unique, specific risks and benefits can vary, and the best choice depends on individual circumstances.

Considering freebirth?

Did you know you can have a birth in the sea or forest? I'm not joking, this has been done. However, most freebirthers do so in their own home, without the assistance of a medical team. Also known as unassisted birth, women may see this as a beautiful way to bring their baby earthside undisturbed, with just them and their chosen people around them. If you're choosing a freebirth, make sure that you really know your shit. It's important to understand the risks alongside the pros: plan it right, do the work, and be radically responsible for your own birth experience.

"It was one of the most empowering and life-changing moments of my life. I breathed my baby our in the pool at home, with no tears and no stitches. Knowledge is power and I'm so thankful."

Water birth

Many of us have an innate urge to birth in water, which is no surprise due to its calming nature. It's also a way women can transition their baby gently from the womb to the world. Babies can be born in water. They receive oxygen through the placenta, allowing for a slow and beautiful birth pause as they adjust to breathing air once out of the water. If the baby starts to emerge on dry land, you'll be encouraged to continue the birth out of the water.

Pros
- Provides instant relief
- Enables spontaneous movement
- Can reduce blood pressure
- Reduces perineal trauma, meaning fewer tears and episiotomies (see page 149).
- Lower intervention rates
- Natural pain relief
- Lowers the stress hormone
- Feels safe and secure
- Gentle transition for baby

Cons
- Some may not enjoy the water
- Would need to leave water for some pain relief options
- Getting into the pool too early could potentially slow down labour

REMINDER
A water birth can be done at home. Just hire or purchase a pool – some even come with a handy drinks holder! #winning

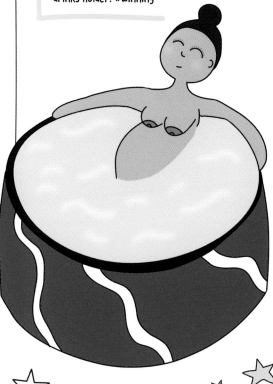

Tip: *Maintain the water temperature at something you're comfortable with – usually around 37°C (99°F).*

You have a right to a midwife-led birth regardless of your situation.

Birth centre/midwife-led unit

This is a great choice if home birth just isn't your thing. Birth centres and other midwife-led units offer a happy medium, but it's important that you're having open and honest discussions with your team. You have every right to a midwife-led birth regardless of your situation or medical condition.

Check your local birth centre/ hospital stats and get a feel for how they're supporting similar births. Places really do vary. Some have low transfer rates, induction or C-sections, while others show high numbers, which is a red flag if you're looking to avoid intervention.

HIGH RISK? STUDIES SHOW THAT HIGH-RISK PREGNANCIES HAVE BETTER OUTCOMES WITH MIDWIFE-LED CARE.

Pros
- Personalised and holistic approach
- Considers the emotional and social aspects alongside the physical
- Less medical Intervention than labour ward
- Less clinical and usually more home-/spa-like
- Midwife-led care supporting vaginal birth

Cons
- Higher intervention rates than home but less than obstetrics/ labour ward
- Possibility of pushback on choices – communication is key
- Need to transfer for induction, epidural, or assisted birth

Labour/obstetrics ward

A labour ward is headed up by consultants who usually oversee high-risk pregnancies, inductions, and transfers for assisted births. It's by choice whether you decide to give birth here, as naturally it does come with an increased rate of intervention. Some find comfort in knowing medical help and epidurals are on hand.

Find an obstetrician who supports physiological birth regardless of if you're choosing vaginal, induction, or C-section. Start by asking around for recommendations from your network and reading online reviews.

Pros
- Immediate emergency care if needed
- Wide range of pain management options
- May be suitable for specialist cases

Cons
- Clinical environment
- Higher rates of medical intervention
- Less personalised experience
- Cost - depending on medical care and where you live
- Possible pushback on choices - communication is key
- Limited mobility in some cases

Schedule consultations to ask about their experience with physiological births, intervention rates, and what the hospital's policies are. Make sure you're comfortable with them and that they share your philosophy for your birth. Don't forget to double-check insurance and costs if that applies to you. Trust your gut feeling – if you feel supported and at ease, you're likely making the right choice. It's essential to find an obstetrician to guide you through the process who not only respects your wishes but is also experienced in physiological birth.

Tip: *Have open and honest convos from the start to ensure you build a supportive relationship.*

Hiring a doula

Your ultimate family advocate and oxytocin superhero. Doulas are there to support you and they come with a whole load of benefits.

Doulas aren't a luxury in my eyes, they are a necessity. They range in cost: some exchange services, some are volunteers. A doula is not the same as a midwife, and they aren't there to replace a birth partner! A doula guarantees continuity of care, which sadly most women don't receive. Having someone to trust and who can help you to make informed decisions is game-changing for your birth experience.

Let's start with a myth: a doula is for "natural" birth only. Nope! Doulas support all types of births, at home, at hospital, and even Caesareans. Remember – your birth isn't about anyone else, it's ultimately about you and your desires. A good doula will support you on your journey and they'll never tell you what you should, or shouldn't, be doing. They're not there for advice but for pure, unwavering support. Each one is unique and has a different skill set. Finding one that aligns with you can be hard, but talk to many and choose someone who you feel an instant spark with.

What about the benefits? Well, these birth superheroes can reduce your risk of induction, instrumental, and Caesarean birth, along with lowering the need for painkillers or an epidural. They also increase your chance of a shorter labour, parental satisfaction with your birth experience, and the likelihood of initiating breastfeeding. Stats show they also lower the chances of postpartum depression, improve equity, and provide culturally responsive care.

Hiring an independent midwife

An independent midwife provides personalised, one-on-one care throughout your pregnancy, labour, and postpartum period. Unlike a hospital setting, where you may meet different healthcare providers, an independent midwife offers continuity of care. They're there to offer advice, provide medical assessments, and give you the emotional support you need. They work in tandem with your medical team to ensure you and your baby are healthy and happy. Why hire one? Because you're worth it. Independent midwives offer a level of personalised care and continuity that can make your entire birth experience more comfortable, less stressful, and possibly quicker. From prenatal to postpartum, they've got you covered, helping you make informed decisions every step of the way.

What else can they offer? Unlike generic care through the healthcare system, an independent midwife can

REMINDER

When choosing a private midwife make sure the vibe between you feels natural and friendly. You want to trust them and be working together on preparing for a super birth experience!

tailor advice and support based on your unique needs and preferences. They are usually experts in natural birthing techniques that can lower the need for intervention.

A lot of independent midwives have a holistic background. They understand the whole process of birth and how to support you during labour through positioning, alternatives to mainstream pain relief and immediate help with initiating breastfeeding. Continued support can also lower the chance of postpartum depression.

 Doulas support all types of births, at home, at hospital, and even Caesareans.

Special considerations in your plan

These are just some personal aspects of your story or identity you may want to include in your birth vision. They should be mentioned to your team ahead of time, and utmost care should be taken to protect your privacy.

Multiples (e.g. twins, triplets)

If you're expecting multiples you still have choices. It's important that you're still advocating for a birth of your choice and discussing how your team can support you to make this happen, whether that's a home birth, vaginal, or C-section.

Religion

Ask for specific practices or traditions before, during, or after birth. Note any dietary restrictions to be respected. Discuss modesty requirements and needs for prayer. Detail any extra support needed.

Rhesus negative

Discuss the plan for anti-D prophylaxis to prevent complications. If foetal RHD genotyping is considered, samples can be taken from the placenta without affecting optimal cord clamping.

Neurodiversity

Your needs should be clearly stated, whether favouring written methods or visual aids. Any sensitivities like light or sound should be detailed, along with strategies to mitigate them. A sense of structure should be maintained to minimise anxiety.

Placenta Previa

Placenta previa is where the placenta partially or completely covers the cervix. Most placentas do move upwards and pose no risk, although you may be asked for closer monitoring, which is up to you. If later on in your pregnancy the placenta has not moved, a C-section is often recommended to ensure a safe birth.

Precipitous labour

This is a labour that progresses extremely rapidly, lasting less than three hours after contractions start. If you have a history of fast labours, it is important to discuss this with your care team and make a plan of action. For example, there's the practical concern of getting to the hospital in time for the birth. The more confident and calm you feel, the better. Consider planning a home birth and having extra support.

Same-sex couples

Sadly, many care providers won't always ask about the person you've brought with you and may assume they are a relative or friend. Pop it on the top of your birth plan so your care team can address your partner correctly.

Breech birth

Breech is when a baby is positioned feet or bum first, rather than headfirst, in the womb. There are several types of breech position, including frank, complete, and footling, each with its own considerations. If your baby is breech, don't panic, there is still time for baby to turn. Consider holistic methods such as Spinning Babies®, moxibustion, or hypnosis. An external cephalic version (ECV) may be offered to turn the babe manually. It's your choice, and is not always successful. While a C-section is often recommended for breech births, vaginal breech birth is still an option under specific conditions. It's crucial to have a healthcare provider skilled in vaginal breech delivery, and be sure to discuss monitoring options to keep tabs on the baby's well-being.

Birth moon and "false starts"

You're getting closer to meeting your babe and it's a game of "is or isn't it"! This is the perfect time for the Naked Doula birth moon.

As you approach or pass the 40-week mark in your journey, it's common to feel anticipation, impatience, and excitement. You've just grown a baby over the last 8, 9, or even 10 months and you're close to meeting them! Let go of the pressure of time and allow yourself to connect with your impending birth in a way that allows your body to be in a state of calm but ready.

Reflect on positive memories: Revisit cherished photos and memories.

Movie nights: Enjoy favourite films, comedy specials or series.

Dance and movement: Use music to connect with your body.

Intimacy and pleasure: Enjoy moments of intimacy and self-pleasure.

Oxytocin boost: Engage in hugging, cuddling or kissing.

Letter to your baby: Write a heartfelt letter to your little one.

Organise baby's things: Sort through and organise baby's belongings.

Talk to your baby: Have conversations and share your excitement.

Get out in nature: Inhale fresh air and get comfort from familiar places.

False starts – false info, babes!

I call bullshit. Dismiss the idea of a "false start" right away, because there's no such thing. Your body is an engine warming up. It's perfectly in tune with what it's doing, and when it gives you signs, no matter how intermittent, cherish them! Embrace the changes, and trust the beautiful and natural process unfolding at its own unique pace.

- **Trust your body:** It is incredibly intelligent and always working in your best interest.

- **Exciting changes:** When labour starts and stops, it's an exciting sign of progress.

- **Welcome niggles:** Welcome the little contractions, and allow them to come and go.

- **No rush:** Don't rush the birthing process; it's unique and doesn't follow a linear path.

- **Hollywood myths:** Hollywood's portrayal of waters breaking and immediate birth is far from reality.

- **Rare event:** Only about 10% of women experience waters breaking before labour begins.

Trust the process: Let labour unfold naturally, rest when needed, and trust your intuition.

- **Consult with the care team:** If anything feels off, consult your midwife or care team for guidance.

- **Hold confidence:** Have confidence in yourself and your body throughout this incredible journey.

REMINDER
You're not a traffic light operating on fixed signals! Let things flow naturally, rest when needed, and enjoy your day while trusting the journey.

Labour imminent?

 Is this really it? Here are some handy signs that may indicate labour is really starting.

The day has finally come. But don't start the party too soon! Once we start noticing things and know that labour is officially starting, we tend to go a bit OTT. Jumping around, staying awake, and doing our best to hurry things along. The bad news about this is that it can wear the body out very fast, leading to fatigue and the inability to handle things when they pick up. So LISTEN to your body, rest, sleep, and eat. What if it starts when you're out and about? Don't panic babe!

Clues

- Clearouts. Poo and lots more poo!
- Pressure in lower back or bum.
- The urge to purge! Extreme need to clean, organise, tidy etc.
- Sudden burst of energy or a complete need to just SLEEP.
- Loss of your mucus plug, in bits or all at once.
- Abdominal pains and tightenings.
- Waters break – only happens to 10% of women.
- Just can't get comfortable. Nothing you do helps!

Depending on baby's position, contractions may feel like period pain or lower back pain. Some feel it more than others. But you've got this, babe! Work with that body!

When to let your midwife know?

Usually when contractions are lasting for 60 seconds and coming every five minutes. Try to stay in a calm environment for as long as possible. Driving to hospital? Use an eye mask, earphones, and comfy pillow to keep oxytocin vibes HIGH!

Tip: *Need to cry? Cry! Need to shout? Shout! LET IT OUT and let it go. Not only does crying release oxytocin but allowing ourselves to speak our worries out loud also has an impact on how our body feels and can help to start the labour process.*

WARNING SIGNS

Here are some of the main things to look out for during pregnancy and early labour to detect pre-eclampsia and other complications. Contact your care provider immediately if you experience these or are worried about your or your baby's well-being.

Baby's movement stopping or slowing during pregnancy	Fever of 38°C (100°F) or higher	Chest pain or fast-beating heart
Severe belly pain that doesn't go away 	Heavy vaginal bleeding	Changes in your vision
Headache that won't go away or gets worse over time	Severe swelling, redness, or pain of your leg or arm	Extreme swelling of your hands or face
Trouble breathing 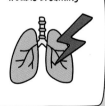	Continuous high blood pressure 	Unexplained nausea and vomiting 

Induction looming!

Induction is a medical process used to initiate contractions artificially before they begin naturally and can be carried out using various methods.

In the conversations I have about birth, induction of labour ALWAYS comes up. Understanding your options, along with your individual circumstances, can help you make informed decisions that feel best for you. It's important to understand the pros and cons associated with induced labour. Induction should only be for medical reasons, not for convenience or impatience, though I understand the feeling. Due dates are often inaccurate: "full term" at 37+ weeks can be misleading, and early induction can do more harm than good as your baby is still developing. So, ask questions and remember you always have the choice to say no.

Induction shouldn't be routinely offered for:

- Suspected big baby
- History of fast labours
- Breech or transverse
- Previous Caesarean
- Well-managed gestational diabetes
- BMI or maternal age with no health concerns
- Healthy IVF babies
- Ending pregnancy early without a valid reason
- If you and baby are well and healthy

It may be considered for:

- Pre-eclampsia
- Other medical conditions

What the research says

An extensive study of over 47,000 births across 16 years revealed that labour induction led to increased intervention for some births including use of forceps, C-sections, episiotomies, and postpartum bleeding in mothers compared to those who went into labour naturally.

REMINDER

You ultimately hold the cards and should make an informed decision that feels right for you. If that is an induction, then remember you can INFLUENCE it in every way!

Babies born from induced labour faced a bumpier start, with increased neonatal intensive care unit stays, traumas, and respiratory issues. In the long term, these infants had more hospital visits for infections, mainly targeting the ear, nose, and throat. The study found no benefits for babies born through unnecessary induction.

Supercervix sweep?

Membrane sweeps are often offered near the end of pregnancy to get things going. This is still a form of induction and can cause irritation and result in a pissed-off cervix. A finger will go into your cervix and sweep around to try to stimulate the release of prostaglandin. It's not always effective and has a risk of infection. It is more effective the further along you are post 40 weeks, but always go with what feels good for you.

Things to consider

Induction might not produce immediate results; contractions may differ from the usual pattern and can be more continuous and intense.

Tip: *A positive induction is possible. Use your body, floppy face, floppy fanny, and set the scene of your environment. You've got this, babe!*

Artificial oxytocin doesn't have the same effects as natural oxytocin, which triggers the release of endorphins. If you opt for this path, remember to apply the techniques from the Body chapter.

QUESTIONS TO ASK

- Any current concerns about my or my baby's well-being?
- Reasons for considering x-week induction for my baby?
- Benefits of x-week induction for me and my baby?
- Long-term effects of induced labour on me and my baby?
- Success rate for inductions at this pregnancy stage?
- Estimated duration from induction to active labour?
- Options if induction is unsuccessful?
- Risks of waiting for natural labour?
- Risks of opting for a planned Caesarean?
- How will I monitor my baby's well-being with a delayed labour decision?

Methods of induction

Dilapan rods

These rods are unique because they absorb cervical moisture, swelling and pressuring the cervix over 12–24 hours. This mechanical process helps the cervix soften and open, potentially starting contractions. **Pros:** predictable dilation, drug-free, suitable for vaginal births after C-section. **Cons:** possible discomfort, time-consuming, slight infection risk, labour may not start right after removal.

Foley balloon

This catheter is another non-hormonal way to induce labour by gently opening the cervix. It's a good choice if you want to avoid hormones and if you've had a previous C-section. The process involves inserting a sterile catheter, inflating a balloon with sterile liquid, and monitoring until enough dilation occurs. **Pros:** no hormones, reversible, gradual dilation **Cons:** discomfort during insertion, slower dilation, slight infection risk.

Prostaglandins

Artificial Prostaglandins are used to ripen the cervix and induce labour, and are administered vaginally in gel or tablet form. **Pros:** effective labour initiation if your body is ready **Cons:** risks of uterine hyperstimulation, potential for increased medical interventions, physical discomfort.

Artificial oxytocin

Given via a drip, artificial oxytocin, like Pitocin or Syntocinon, is a synthetic hormone used to start or strengthen labour. The pros are that you can ask for a lower dose to start and even come off it if things kick off. It does come with the risk of hyperstimulation, which could affect baby's oxygen supply and potentially lead to a C-section. It also requires more monitoring to prevent problems like maternal fluid retention and can cause more intense and unnatural contractions. This method can also mess with the natural flow of your own body's hormone transmission.

Breaking waters

Breaking waters, or AROM (Artificial Rupture of Membranes), is a method that involves puncturing your amniotic sac to initiate or speed up labour. It's important to know that the amniotic sac serves as protection and a cushion for your baby. Removing the waters during an induction is standard practice but can be risky for non-induced birth and result in a rapid increase in the intensity of contractions and intervention. While it may encourage natural labour, there are risks such as infection for both the mother and baby, rare umbilical cord issues, and the possibility that it might not work.

Natural induction: Busting myths

The term "natural induction" has gained significant traction among parents-to-be who prefer a less medicalised approach. From consuming spicy foods and pineapple to having sex, there are plenty of suggested methods out there promising to initiate labour naturally. However, I'm calling BS! Trying to force labour, especially with methods such as castor oil, can be really dangerous. The truth is, babies come when babies come, and while you can definitely help to initiate labour with oxytocin-loving activities like the Naked Doula birth moon and movement, only when your body is ready will anything make a difference. Remember, your body is warming up like a finely tuned engine and it's getting ready for the big event! Even medical induction methods like the ones I've described can take days to kick in, so take a breather and make patience your friend. If you've already started dilating or things are moving along, think about taking a pass on medical induction and give your body a chance to do what it's made to do. You always have the option to change your unique journey at any time. Your body, your birth, your choice.

Stages of labour

Textbooks tell us labour and birth should go a certain way, but from experience this isn't the case! We are all UNIQUE and so is our pregnancy and birth. Regardless of where you start, stop, or find yourself, here is the lowdown on what those stages may look and feel like.

Warming up the engines
- Little niggles, pains, or distractions
- Clearouts, loss of mucus plug, bloody show
- Back ache, Braxton Hicks contractions
- Uncomfortable, tired, or bursts of energy

What we think it looks like

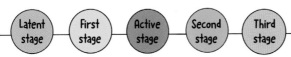

Latent stage — First stage — Active stage — Second stage — Third stage

What it could look like

Stop/start

Early labour: Dilation and effacement of the cervix

Early labour
- The cervix begins to dilate (open) and efface (thin out).
- Contractions start out mild and infrequent but gradually become more regular.
- This phase is typically the longest but is usually less intense than active labour.

Established labour
- The cervix dilates more rapidly, from about 4cm (1½in) to 7cm (2¾in).
- Contractions are stronger, more frequent, and more regular.
- Comfort measures and support may become more needed during this phase.

Second stage: Birth of the baby

Pushing:
- Once the cervix is fully dilated, you will start to feel a strong urge to push.
- With each contraction, you will bear down.
- The head starts to descend through the birth canal and "crowns" when the widest part is at the vaginal opening.

Birth:
- After the head is born, mum might want to touch and take time before the baby rotates and the shoulders are out.
- Once the shoulders are born, the rest of the body usually follows quickly.
- Mum can then immediately bring the baby to chest, or pause first before skin-to-skin contact.

Transition phase

- The cervix dilates.
- Contractions may feel very strong, lasting about 60–90 seconds and occurring every 2–3 minutes.
- This is often the most challenging phase but is also the shortest.

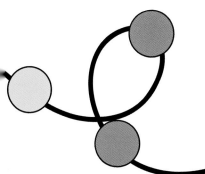

Third stage: Birth of the placenta

- After the baby is born, the uterus continues to contract to expel the placenta.
- This usually occurs within 5–60 minutes post birth, sometimes longer.
- It's essential that the entire placenta is expelled to prevent complications – think oxytocin and plenty of skin-to-skin.

Labour tricks and extra bits

Your body knows what to do and oxytocin will flow regardless during labour. However, these are a few things that may help keep you in the flow!

Sloth progress?

What happens if everything has been feeling fricking fantastic, but all of a sudden slows down? This is a normal phenomenon. But listen carefully as it may be a sign that something in your space isn't right!

Think environment

Has it become noisy, bright, or distracting? Swap it up for some privacy, stick your earphones in, and dim the light – or use an eye mask.

Think brain

How do you feel? Are you feeling anxious or scared? Fear can affect that queen bee oxytocin. Speak your fears out loud, and use the practical exercises on pages 40-41.

Think body

Are you comfortable? Do you feel restricted? Or maybe you're lying down when you'd rather be up? Feel what your body needs and change it up.

Intervention prevention

Your body is working damn hard and you know that it's doing exactly what it needs to do. Every time you feel that doubt, lean into your gut and intuition. You know your body and what it's feeling better than anyone else babe, trust me! But there are a few little but important bits that you may want to keep in mind...

REMINDER

Intervention isn't always the enemy, but it has to feel right for you.

Stay hydrated

Water is your best mate, but not too much! Think of it like a marathon: you need to stay hydrated but not so full you're about to burst. Dehydration may lead to needing IV fluids.

Make sure you wee

Water in means water out. Don't forget to wee! A full bladder might reduce space for baby to descend.

Lose the clock

Taking more time doesn't have to mean intervention. Don't feel pressured into doing something within a time limit. Remember that labour is not linear and being under pressure can slow things down or even stop labour altogether.

A little help

If you find yourself dehydrated, needing a catheter due to a bladder that wants a little help, or an epidural to take the edge off, do not fear! You can still influence your environment, positions, and movement.

Catheter

A catheter is commonly used with epidurals or toilet issues, helping to avoid urinary retention. While effective, it can cause discomfort and limit movement.

IV fluids

An IV line in labour offers fast fluid and medication delivery, aiding hydration and emergencies. Though it is generally safe, it may cause discomfort, limit movement, and increase risk of infection.

CTG monitoring

Cardiotocography tracks the baby's heart rate with sensors, usually on your belly. It's used to detect foetal distress. It is not always accurate due to movement, and positioning it may trigger unnecessary interventions, limit movement, and add stress.

Intermittent monitoring

Instead of constant surveillance of baby's heart rate and your contractions, sensors are applied at intervals, or a handheld monitor is used to capture data. This allows for greater freedom of movement and a less clinical atmosphere.

The ideal environment

You can influence your environment no matter where or how you birth. Your baby holds the key.

Environment is key to a positive experience because it impacts how you feel. The more comfortable you are, the more you can tune into your body. A little secret is that your baby actually has the key to the perfect environment. Picture this: floating around, you feel loved and safe, able to move freely, surrounded by darkness with a red tone, nutrients, and water, and you are snug as a bug. Warm, cosy, and extremely happy... Well that's an indication of how you might like to set up your environment. Think of yourself in a big old womb. This can be created pretty much anywhere. Even on a labour ward, you still have choices and options!

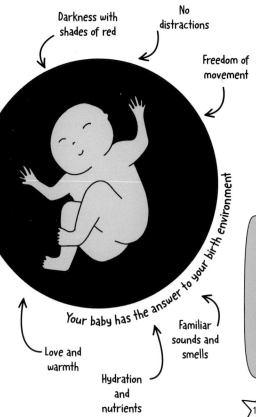

Darkness with shades of red

No distractions

Freedom of movement

Your baby has the answer to your birth environment

Familiar sounds and smells

Love and warmth

Hydration and nutrients

Creating your perfect environment

- Pillow
- Blanket
- Sentimental items
- Photos
- Lights
- Pregnancy pillow
- Earphones
- Eye mask
- Lighting
- Privacy
- Music
- Comfort
- Equipment hidden or moved

Birth partners 101

The birth partner is paramount to a successful birth. As a partner, you can understand your role by embracing each of these birth partner superpowers.

Enviroman - Balls of Steel (no actual testicles required)

About Enviroman is the leader in birth environments. He knows how imperative it is to get the environment right. Enviroman is an advocate for his birth partner and ensures that things feel homely and comfortable. The right environment lowers the chances of intervention, including Caesarean section.

Powers: darkness / no distractions / home comforts / do not disturb / music / safe spaces

DISLIKES: BRIGHT LIGHTS

Supportia - The Mindful Angel

About Supportia is all about support during labour and birth. Support in choice but also support in what is needed at that time. It's your job to be there if needed but to back off and stay away if not. Be mindful of what's going on and ensure you are listening. The more we listen, the more we can be mindful about what is needed from us.

Powers: mindfulness / hands off or on / listening / supporting choice / creating ease / holding space

DISLIKES: BEING IGNORED

Planaman - Knows His Shit

About Birth planning is THE BEST! Not only does it help you both learn about what to expect but also allows you to decide what you're open-minded about and what you definitely are not. It helps you have a sense of control and allows your caregivers to help you achieve your goals. Use the B.R.A.I.N. acronym (see page 114) for all your decisions.

Powers: supporting plans / gatekeeping / birth rights / advocating / B.R.A.I.N. / knowledge

DISLIKES: NOT BEING INFORMED

Oxytocina - Queen of Birth

About Oxytocina is the guardian of oxytocin, one of the most important things during labour as this is the hormone driving it. Fear = tension = pain = interventions. So embrace this superhero with both arms and get your game face on! OXYTOCIN IS KEY.

Powers: love / laughter / safety and privacy / being informed / happiness / positive language / pain relief and comfort measures / non-medical options

DISLIKES: FEAR

141

Pain relief piggy bank

This piggy knows the importance of comfort. Here are some non-medical ways to have in your toolkit if you're after a drug-free birth experience.

Breathwork

Don't underestimate the natural tool of deep, rhythmic breathing during labour. It not only gives you focus but also oxygenates the blood and relaxes your muscles, making contractions easier to handle. Inhale deeply through your nose, let your abdomen rise as you fill your lungs, and then exhale completely through your mouth. This controlled breathing is like a charm that steadies your mind and body, helping you manage intense moments.

Floppy Face, Floppy Fanny

Don't forget about the most talked-about technique in every birth story! This beauty is the difference between fighting against and working with those contractions. So remember to drop your jaw and face and allow those shoulders to follow. The more you can relax your face, the more your pelvic floor will relax, offering space for your uterus and less intense surges.

Movement

Movement during labour, like walking, swaying, changing positions, or our famous dancing, can be a simple yet effective way to manage pain and facilitate the labour process. By enhancing blood circulation and optimising the baby's position, movement can make contractions more efficient and possibly shorter.

The birth comb and acupressure

Squeezing a birth comb is like having a superpower. It not only diverts your brain from the sensation of contractions, but it also stimulates the vagus nerve to release feel-good hormones. Hold a comb so its teeth press into your palm's base during contractions, and relax your grip in between. I recommend The Wave Comb for ultimate birth comb vibes! Tightly grasping the teeth of a comb activates nerve endings in your hands, distracting your brain from the pain of contractions. It's like tricking your brain into paying attention to the hand rather than the intense action in your uterus.

Massage and touching

Embracing the power of touch through massage and counterpressure can be a real game-changer. If you have a birth partner, they can act as your masseur, kneading tension away from your back, hips, or any other area that needs soothing. This hands-on approach helps alleviate pain and creates an intimate, comforting atmosphere. A popular technique is the hip squeeze. And don't forget all that oxytocin that will be flowing through all that touching.

Aromatherapy

Aromatherapy brings a touch of spa-like serenity to the labour room. This natural approach uses essential oils like lavender, chamomile, or frankincense to create a soothing atmosphere that can help you relax both physically and mentally. Clary sage is powerful and should be used lightly. A few drops on a cotton ball or flannel can go a long way in reducing anxiety and enhancing your emotional well-being. Always consult your healthcare provider first to ensure the scents you choose are safe for you and your baby.

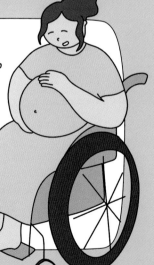

Need a little support?

You should never be denied pain relief should you ask for it. Here are a range of options that are there if you need that extra support.

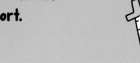

Paracetamol

Paracetamol can be used for mild to moderate relief at any time during labour. It's easily accessible and can provide relief for 2–3 hours. However, as labour progresses, it may become less effective and could potentially interfere with natural labour progression. Rare side effects like nausea and drowsiness are possible, and it's advised to avoid codeine variants if planning to breastfeed. Always follow the recommended dosage and consult your healthcare provider for personalised recommendations.

Sterile water injections

Sterile water injections offer a drug-free alternative to traditional comfort measures, providing relief, particularly for pesky back pain. While the initial injections might sting, many report quick relief. It's a bit of a rare gem, not offered everywhere, but if available and suitable for you, it could be just the ticket for dodging medication and its potential side effects. The only caveat is that, just like any break of the skin, it comes with a tiny risk of infection.

TENS (transcutaneous electrical nerve stimulation)

Four pads are placed on your back to send a gentle electrical current through your body. This ticklish sensation helps produce more endorphins and interrupts the pain signals going to your brain. You can adjust the machine to your comfort, and it's especially useful for back labour and early stages of labour. However, it's not a quick fix (it can take a while to kick in), can't be used in water, and may not fully eliminate the sensation.

Gas and air

Entonox, also known as laughing gas, is a blend of nitrous oxide and oxygen you can inhale for relief and reduced anxiety during labour. It's less potent than epidurals and opioids but generally safer and isn't known to hinder natural labour. You control how much and how often you inhale; it acts quickly but also wears off fast. It requires active participation to time the inhalations with contractions and can cause some dizziness or nausea. For best results, start inhaling right before a contraction peaks.

Opioids

Opioids may give you a break but they're not always effective. They're administered usually via injection or IV and are fast to work. However, the bad news is they can cause nausea, drowsiness, and even rare cases of reduced oxygen levels. They might also make your baby sleepy, affect their breathing, and interfere with breastfeeding. Timing and dosage are key here; using them earlier in labour minimises risks, but they do stay in your system for up to 72 hours.

Epidural

An epidural numbs the lower half of your body, blocking pain signals between your body and brain, which is great if you're feeling exhausted! It's highly effective and adjustable, with some opting for a mobile epidural so that they can move around. However, it can lead to lowered blood pressure affecting you and baby, post-delivery headaches, and rare but severe complications like infection or nerve injury. Your mobility may be restricted, and you may require additional interventions, like forceps or artificial oxytocin, to speed up labour. The epidural itself is given using a local anaesthetic and the insertion of a needle and catheter into your spine. Once set, continuous monitoring ensures you and your baby's well-being.

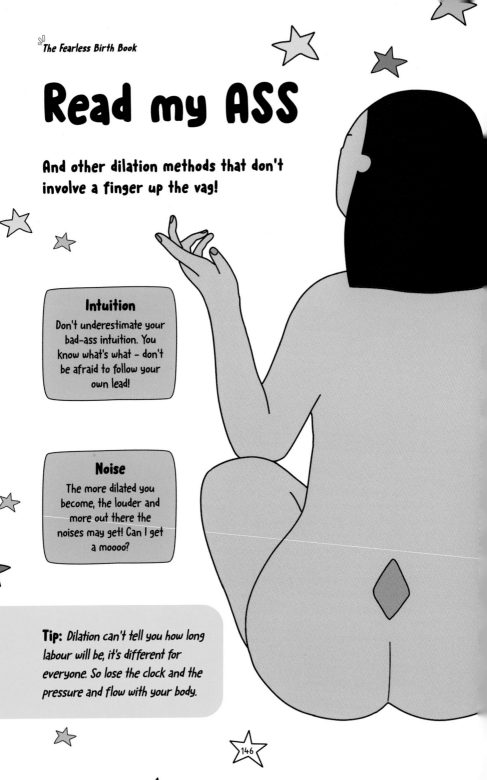

Read my ASS

And other dilation methods that don't involve a finger up the vag!

Intuition
Don't underestimate your bad-ass intuition. You know what's what - don't be afraid to follow your own lead!

Noise
The more dilated you become, the louder and more out there the noises may get! Can I get a moooo?

Tip: *Dilation can't tell you how long labour will be, it's different for everyone. So lose the clock and the pressure and flow with your body.*

Remind yourself about vaginal exams from birth rights expert Emma Ashworth on page 66.

Shit happens and it's a super sign

Worried about pooing? Get ready to flip the script babe! Feeling the urge to poo is a great sign that baby is close. Midwives love seeing this or when you mention it. I like to call them no-shit-ninjas because usually, as fast as the poo happens, they'll clean it up. Plop in the pool? No drama. The sweeping sieve comes in and out like a flash of light!

Zen zone
That hardcore birth zone, when the convo slows down and the focus is real. Active labour is underway.

Diamond dilation
As the sacrum moves outwards to make space, you may see a diamond shape called The Rhombus of Michaelis - baba is imminent!

The buttcrack line
A line, purple on light skin, silver on dark skin. Higher and more prominent as labour progresses! Seen in over 75% of women. Don't worry if this fine line pops up before labour, it's the norm and will change when things get going.

Crowning glory

The moment you've been waiting for! Your babe is just moments away.

Intuitive pushing

Use your breath and send that energy down. Surrender! Avoid gritted teeth and held breath if you can. Opting for intuitive over coached pushing can give you a sense of control, although you may prefer a bit of guidance. The choice is yours.

The ring of fire

This burning sensation only lasts a few seconds. Hands-off is a more natural approach, but if you prefer you can ask your midwife for some perineum support.

Position

You know the score babe, keep that sacrum free, and above all go with what feels best for you. Avoid lying on your back if you want to avoid interventions.

Catching your baby

Babies are born, pizzas are delivered! You get to decide whose arms they're born into. Want to catch your own baby? Cool! Birth partner ready? Yes! Prefer the midwife? They'll be right there for you.

Tearing

Your perineum is designed to stretch and tear if needed. You don't usually even notice. Using FFFF and breathwork can make it less likely to tear.

Go back to page 90 to remind yourself of all the juicy positions to birth your babe.

REMINDER

No need to rush, babe!
Allow those pauses for
your body to stretch
and move.

Need a hand?

You may dream of a hands-off
birth but don't beat yourself up if
you need some help. These are
some of the interventions that may
be offered. An **episiotomy** is a cut
to the perineum. It should only be
used in real emergencies as it can
increase the chance of a worse
tear. **Forceps** and **vacuum suction**
are tools used when things stop or
there are signs of distress in the
baby. They shouldn't be used as a
time limit tool! Forceps look like
large spoons and help guide the
baby out of the birth canal,
offering a faster alternative to a
C-section. **Vacuum extraction**,
also called ventouse, uses
suction and is seen as a less
invasive option than forceps and
may carry a reduced risk of
maternal injury. However, there
are still risks, including
potential injuries to baby.
Foetal scalp electrode
is a monitoring option
where a tiny
corkscrew-type
monitor is attached
to the baby's head. It
hasn't been shown to
decrease complications.

You did it!

You birthed your baby into the world! You are amazing. Your oxytocin levels are the highest they'll ever be!

Wiping baby

Your baby is most likely covered in vernix. This is a MAGIC white antimicrobial substance that blocks shitty bacteria. It helps you to bond and moisturises baby's skin. If you gave birth vaginally, your baby also has a microbiome from your vaginal canal, which is invaluable for first immunity. You may see a little blood – that's okay. Gently wipe away and relax.

Baby colour

It's normal for your baby to be purple or dark red, this usually changes within a few minutes but can sometimes take longer as baby transitions earthside. Remember, while the cord is still pulsating, they're getting oxygen. Skin-to-skin also helps.

Newborn babies don't need to be vigorously rubbed or pinched to get them to cry or move. Newborns are smart beings who do not always cry at birth. It isn't necessary to clear a baby's lungs and some might not cry at all. Give them time.

Delayed checks

To avoid separating you and baby, checks can be delayed, including things like weight. Your care provider can observe baby while they're on you and there is no need for them to be taken away without your consent.

Eye gel

In the US an antibiotic gel is used routinely in case of STDs passed on from the mother's vaginal canal. This is rare, and baby is well-protected within their vernix. If you know you're STD-free you may want to opt out of this as it can obscure baby's vision and disrupt bonding.

Apgar scores

This is a score that your care provider uses to monitor baby when they're born. A 7, 8, or 9 is normal and is a sign that the newborn is in good health. The number usually rises within a few minutes. You have the right to stay with your baby at all times regardless of the circumstances.

Vitamin K

All babies are born with low levels of vitamin K, rising to the norm around day 12. To avoid the rare case of VKDB (Vitamin K deficiency bleeding), the shot, a synthetic version, is given via injection instantly or orally over three weeks. This is not mandatory, so you can opt out if you prefer. The injection can cause some pain and bruising for baby, while the oral dose is less invasive. However, you would have to administer the second and third doses yourself. Breastfeed while it's being given as this offers natural pain relief.

Emergencies

Preparing for unexpected emergencies can provide peace of mind. Ensure that resuscitation equipment is readily available for any necessary interventions. Create a plan for your partner to maintain skin-to-skin contact with the baby, especially if you're separated for any reason. If you undergo general anaesthesia, request delayed cord clamping and skin-to-skin contact in the operating theatre when possible. Also, discuss the option to keep the umbilical cord attached longer, as it can continue supplying oxygen if the baby requires breathing support. Having these plans in place ensures you're well prepared for any unexpected surprises.

IN SOME CULTURES, PUTTING YOUR MOUTH OVER THE NOSE AND MOUTH OF THE BABY TO SUCK ANY EXCESS LIQUID FROM THE LUNGS IS USED, RATHER THAN MEDICAL SUCTION EQUIPMENT.

The Golden Hour

The Golden Hour is the first magical 60 minutes (or much more if poss) after birth. It sets the stage for a lifelong bond.

This is the time to soak up your baby, with hours of skin-to-skin contact, breastfeeding initiation, and relaxation. This time can be game-changing, although not everyone will feel like this or get to experience it. If that's you, don't forget that bonding is a process and is not always instant.

Wait for white

Optimal and delayed cord clamping is incredibly beneficial for newborns, especially those born prematurely. By waiting for the cord to turn white, several advantages are achieved for the baby. These include a 30% increase in blood volume, improved levels of haemoglobin, higher blood pressure, enhanced cerebral

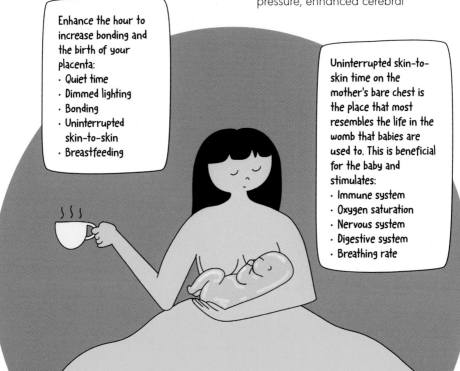

Enhance the hour to increase bonding and the birth of your placenta:
· Quiet time
· Dimmed lighting
· Bonding
· Uninterrupted skin-to-skin
· Breastfeeding

Uninterrupted skin-to-skin time on the mother's bare chest is the place that most resembles the life in the womb that babies are used to. This is beneficial for the baby and stimulates:
· Immune system
· Oxygen saturation
· Nervous system
· Digestive system
· Breathing rate

oxygenation, better flow of red blood cells, extended breastfeeding duration, increased stem cell volume, and a stronger immune system. Furthermore, this practice reduces the risk of various complications like brain haemorrhages, enterocolitis, late-onset sepsis, the need for blood transfusions or anaemia, the need for mechanical ventilation, and umbilical infections. Delayed cord clamping is a simple yet powerful way to promote the health and well-being of newborns, particularly premature infants.

Birthing your placenta

The birth of your placenta deserves as much attention and honour as the birth itself. Data suggests that active management of the third stage of labour following a physiological birth may increase the risk of significant blood loss. So, much like the act of giving birth, the third stage should be approached with a high degree of care and informed consent.

Things that help birth the placenta

Oxytocin, skin-to-skin, breastfeeding, and even sitting on the loo! Yes this works like a dream (use a commode to catch it). Don't forget to breathe your placenta out. Hands-off works best – no one should be pulling on placenta. Fundal massage is not necessary unless in an emergency. Use the trusty birth comb for afterpains.

What can I do with it?

Some choose to keep the placenta, preserving it through processes like plastination. There is a growing trend of encapsulating the placenta into tablets, thought to have health benefits, although scientific evidence is limited. Others may opt to include the placenta in a ceremonial practice. Whether you wish to see it, keep it, or use it for ceremonial or health reasons, the choice is yours, and healthcare providers are increasingly open to honouring these personal preferences.

Not every mum and baby will get a golden hour, especially those who need support in NICU. You can still create a plan with your care provider to have regular skin-to-skin alongside feeding, while also using methods like singing and reading stories to build a bond with your newborn.

Vaginal birth after Caesarean

Preparing for a VBAC may feel overwhelming. Here are some fast facts to help you achieve your goals.

A VBAC (Vaginal Birth After Caesarean) can be a deeply empowering experience. It's vital to be well-informed and take specific measures to increase the chances of a successful VBAC. Gather information from a variety of credible sources, including your healthcare provider, to understand the pros and cons of attempting a VBAC versus opting for a repeat C-section.

Choose the right healthcare provider

- **Experience matters** Opt for a healthcare provider experienced in handling VBACs.
- **Collaborative care** Your provider should respect your birth plan and be open to discussion about your preferred VBAC approach.

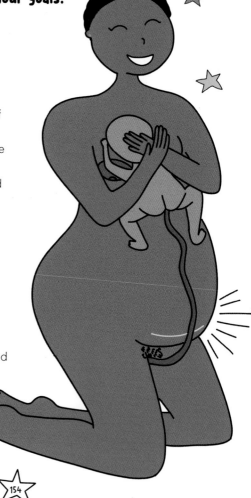

Keep interventions to a minimum (hands-off approach)

- **Opt for spontaneous labour** Letting labour begin naturally can increase the chances of a successful VBAC.
- **Informed waiting** In cases where labour isn't progressing, consult your healthcare provider about the benefits and risks of waiting versus intervening.
- **Natural progression** Allowing labour to progress naturally minimises the need for interventions like Pitocin, which can complicate a VBAC.
- **Informed consent** Make sure to fully understand any proposed interventions, their risks, and their alternatives before giving consent.

Consider water birth or labouring in water

- **Pain relief** The buoyancy and warmth of water can serve as a natural pain relief method.
- **Enhanced mobility** Being in water may make it easier to change positions, which can aid the progress of labour.

Trust your body

- **Mindfulness and relaxation** Techniques such as deep breathing and visualisation can help you stay relaxed, which is crucial for labour progression.
- **Physical preparedness** Light exercise and pelvic floor strengthening may enhance your body's ability to undergo a successful VBAC.

Continuous support

- **Doula support** A doula can provide continuous emotional and physical support, often improving VBAC outcomes.

Conclusion

A positive and powerful VBAC is achievable with the right information, healthcare provider, and birth environment. Remember, every birth experience is unique, so adapt these points to suit your individual needs for the most empowered VBAC possible. Remember to consult with your healthcare provider for personalised advice tailored to your specific medical history and current condition.

 A positive and powerful vaginal birth after C-section is achievable with the right information.

Mother-led Caesarean

Belly birth is beautiful. Find a doctor who will support your choices in creating a positive and gentle birth experience for you and your baby.

Environment

You can have control over your environment in the theatre. Ask for dimmed lights, music, access to pictures etc. The more you do to increase your oxytocin levels and reduce fear and adrenaline, the better.

Skin-to-skin

Baby can be passed to you straight away. By having ECGs placed on your back instead of your front, baby does not have to be taken away from you, as all checks can be delayed.

Delayed cord clamping

A Caesarean lotus birth is where the baby gets delivered with the placenta so the cord remains attached and can be left until it is white. Ask if this is an option for you. The more you delay, the better, even if it is only for a couple of minutes.

Maternal assisted

This is when you deliver your own baby! This is done using gloves. When baby is ready, you simply reach down and pull baby to your chest.

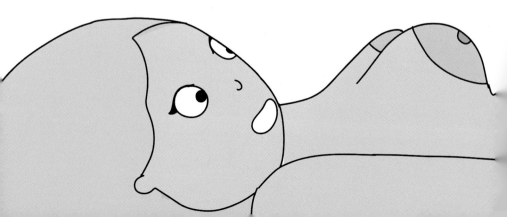

How it happens

A 10-20cm (4-8in) cut is made in the tummy and womb. Baby is birthed within 5-10 mins. The whole procedure usually takes 40-50 minutes. You shouldn't have any food or drink for two hours beforehand but you can sip water. You'll be given a gown and compression socks, and your partner will change into scrubs. Anaesthetic is given, usually by spinal or epidural (general anaesthetic is used in some cases). A catheter will be inserted into your bladder, with consent. You will be given an oxytocin injection, to encourage womb contractions and reduce blood loss. The womb is closed with dissolvable stitches and the tummy is closed with either dissolvable stitches, ordinary stitches, or staples that'll need to be removed a few days after. You'll be moved to a room to recover, offered

painkillers, food, and water, and help with breastfeeding if wanted. The catheter will usually be removed 12-18 hours after the operation. You'll be encouraged to move within the first 24 hours, but take it easy for six weeks or so. Clean the wound every day. Wear loose, comfortable clothes and cotton underwear. Watch out for signs of infection. Ask for help! Contact your midwife or GP if you have any issues, and make sure to rest. The average hospital stay post-op is 2-4 days.

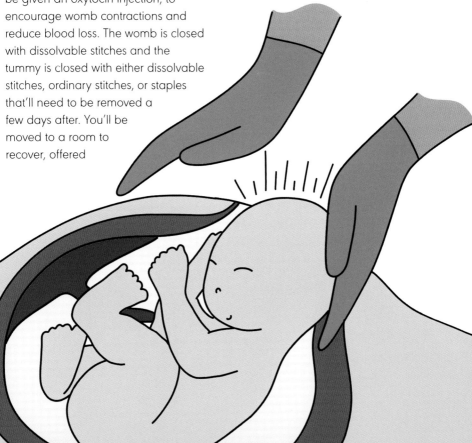

What to expect in theatre

People Anaesthetist, anaesthetic nurse, obstetrician, obstetrician's assistant, midwife, student, scrub nurse, one or two theatre nurses, and paediatrician plus team.

What is it like? Bright lights are pretty standard in a surgical setting, but remember you can ask for dimmed lighting. The team will use a bright spotlight to birth your baby.

What can you see? Your birth partner and the anaesthetist. A screen usually hides everyone else, although you may see people walking by you. You'll see the screen until baby arrives, unless you ask for it to be lowered.

C-section babies & bacteria

Babies born vaginally are coated in and swallow bacteria which has built up throughout pregnancy. When born via C-section they don't get this special group of bacteria.

What can you do? Ask the obstetrician for a vaginal swab, where a gauze is placed inside your vagina to soak up bacteria. This is then placed in a sterile tub. As soon as the baby is born, the gauze is rubbed over the baby. Within a few weeks the similarities between vaginal and Caesarean bacteria is almost identical.

C-section recovery

You may be in hospital for one to four days, but will need to take things easy for several weeks. A catheter will remain in your bladder for at least 12 hours. Your wound will be covered with a dressing for at least 24 hours and you'll be offered painkillers. You'll have regular close contact with your baby and can start breastfeeding. Get out of bed and move around as soon as possible. You can eat and drink as soon as you feel hungry or thirsty.

Returning to your normal activities

Do gentle activities, such as going for a daily walk, to reduce the risk of blood clots. Be careful not to over-exert yourself. You should be able to hold your baby once you get home, but driving, exercising, having sex, and carrying anything heavier than your baby should be avoided. Only do things when you feel able to do so and do not find them uncomfortable. This may not be for six weeks or longer. Ask your midwife for advice if you're unsure of anything at all.

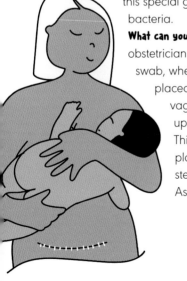

"Being informed is the best
way to reframe your mind
and ditch the fear! I did end up
having a C-section, but it was on
my terms. We had music playing,
essential oils, and made choices
that worked best for us."

Rainbow babies and loss

Acknowledging loss and planning for another baby is difficult. You'll need to manage anxiety while you prepare for the future.

Over a third of us will experience a loss of some kind, whether that's miscarriage, an ectopic, chemical or molar pregnancy, TMFR (termination for medical reasons), neonatal loss, stillbirth, or child loss. Abortion comes under this topic for those who couldn't have their child due to medical conditions or circumstances, or feel conflicted for any reason.

When you've experienced grief in this way it's no wonder you're affected when you fall pregnant again. Worries about losing a child can rob you of the joys of pregnancy and leave you with a feeling of disempowerment during birth, afraid to take control of your decisions out of fear they may be the wrong ones. The truth is, you need to prepare more than ever. Allowing yourself to do the work of reframing, building that brain library, and creating confidence is paramount. And while you can work to cope with it, the anxiety never quite vanishes. Hold on to your bravery and ability to push through and make informed decisions that feel good for you.

A forever bond

During pregnancy, an incredible phenomenon occurs where your baby's cells migrate into your bloodstream and vice versa. This continuous exchange of cells creates a unique connection between you and your child. What's even more astonishing is that these exchanged

DID YOU KNOW?
A RAINBOW BABY IS ONE BIRTHED AFTER A PREVIOUS PREGNANCY OR BABY LOSS.

Hold on to your bravery and ability to push through and make informed decisions.

cells can leave a lasting imprint on your body, including your tissues, bones, brain, and skin, which can persist for decades.

Even if a pregnancy doesn't reach full term, the cells from the developing foetus can still find their way into your bloodstream. Research show that these foetal cells can play a role in healing and regeneration. For example, in cases of heart injury, foetal cells have been observed rushing to the injured area to help mend the heart. Studies have shown the presence of foetal cells in a mother's brain even 18 years after giving birth. This ongoing connection between a mother and her child highlights the remarkable and enduring bond between them.

Preparing for a rainbow baby

Firstly, you're not alone. It may feel lonely to get pregnant again, especially with loss being such a

taboo subject. Secondly, you are brave and your body is more than capable of carrying a child, but you have to nurture brain and body to feel a sense of calm, grounding energy in preparation for the birth. Make sure to mention or discuss your previous loss with your care providers, highlighting a need for sensitivity and mindful use of language. Go for regular walks in nature, and use grounding techniques, breathwork, and rituals to help you feel calm. Connect with your baby daily and try not to dissociate from your experience. Instead lean into it, get a belly cast done, write your baby a letter, or read them stories regularly. Creating your birth plan is especially important for you to feel safe and understand all of your options.

Warning: The next pages are for those experiencing loss.

Birthing your sleeping baby

Powerful support and guidance for expected and unexpected loss, and how to manage grief.

As a mother and a doula I have experienced a lot of loss in my life, including my own early miscarriage. I have also experienced two stillbirths in my career, and the grief of those families will stay with me forever. One thing that rings true in every circumstance is that there is no light without darkness. And when things feel so dark and suffocating, know that light and life are still out there for you. You can do this, you can get through this, and although it may not get easier, you can learn to process your feelings and emotions and honour your baby in so many ways.

REMINDER

You're not alone. Reach out to healthcare providers, support groups, and loved ones to guide you through this experience.

Preparing to birth a sleeping baby

You may be wondering how you can create a positive birth experience when giving birth to a sleeping baby. Although it's hard to comprehend at first, the control of having a plan and creating a special moment can be extremely powerful for both parents. I, like you, also couldn't wrap my head around preparing for such an event after the worst had happened, and it wasn't until a story rolled into my inbox that I understood the true power of this. A lovely couple had written to me and shared the most beautiful story of them birthing their sleeping baby in darkness, with music, hypnobirthing, and FFFF. The mother had used the breathing techniques and even breathed her baby out. They spent time with their angel and created a heartwarming, memorable experience from something that is traumatic. It was at that moment I realised the true beauty of being fearless for birth.

162

Guidance for those expecting loss

Create a loving environment Start by creating a peaceful and loving atmosphere in your birth space. Dim the lights, play soft music, and surround yourself with comforting items that hold significance for you and your family.

Listen to your body Lean into the contractions, use FFFF and the breathing techniques you've learnt. Know that this energy of surrender is connecting with your baby's spirit and making it a sacred experience.

Share the experience If you're comfortable, invite close family members or friends to be with you during the birth. This can provide emotional support and allow them to bond with your baby as well.

Write letters or poems Express your feelings and love for your baby by writing letters or poems. These heartfelt messages can serve as a beautiful way to commemorate your time together.

Guidance for those with unexpected loss

Seek support Reach out to support groups, therapists, or counsellors who specialise in perinatal loss. Connecting with others who have experienced similar situations can be comforting and help you navigate your grief.

Photographs and mementos Capture moments with your baby through photographs and mementos. Many parents find solace in taking pictures of their baby's hands and feet, as well as creating footprints and handprints.

Ceremony and rituals Consider holding a private ceremony to say goodbye to your baby. This can include lighting candles, releasing balloons, or planting a tree in your baby's memory.

Remember self-care Take care of yourself during this time. Take moments to rest, eat, and seek emotional support from loved ones and professionals.

Every family's experience is unique, and there is no right or wrong way to prepare for the birth of a stillborn baby. What matters most is that you create a space filled with love and compassion to honour your baby, and provide yourself with the support you need during this profoundly challenging journey.

BIRTH Key points

You are UNIQUE

Your experience is yours and it won't look the same as anyone else's. So, it's time to forget what Sue and Kara are doing and concentrate on YOUR values, choices, and feelings. Create a flexible plan that fits in with your version of a positive experience.

Birth moon bloom

Hitting the due-date mark can send us into overdrive, but remember, due dates are pretty inaccurate and your baby knows the score. Take this time to create the perfect birth moon and enjoy every feeling or sensation without expectations. The engine is warming, babe!

Induction

This is a big topic with lots of ins and outs! Navigate this with your GUT, ask all the questions and do what feels right for you. Remember, if you choose an induction you can still influence it, utilising all the techniques you've learnt - and don't forget brain buzzers.

Read about brain buzzers, and get ideas for your own set, on page 44.

101

Setting the scene

Your baby has the key to your environment. Set the scene so that you feel comfortable and cosy. Feeling safe and supported will help you focus and go inward. Remember, labour isn't linear and may have its own path; listen to it and tune into what it needs.

Birth partners

You are NEEDED! Don't be a phone-scrolling couch potato, be a birth superhero. This is a time for you to shine, and support their every need. Help set the scene, advocate, and ensure you're following their lead. Stay away from things that may distract them and offer unwavering support.

Pain and comfort

You get to decide what this looks like. You may want to use techniques such as breathing, aromatherapy, or the birth comb. Or you may feel you need a little extra medical help. Either way, know your options and go with what feels right for you.

Birthing your baby

At this point during birth you're deep within the realms of labour. Move with your body, listen to what you need, and get support that feels right. You might want to let your body take over and completely surrender, or get some extra help from your midwife. Your birth, your choice babe.

BABY & BEYOND

Preparing for the post-party period

Congratulations!
You've birthed a baby
into the world and have
gone through the massive
transition into parenthood.
You're probably feeling a
rollercoaster of emotions.
This section is all about
making things simple. Here, we
will debunk myths and cover
newborn needs: the cues,
the poos, and the
unpopular
views!

SHIT you've got a newborn

Have you had the OMG moment yet: looking at your baby and thinking WOW!... but what now? I'm here to navigate the overwhelm with you.

Post-birth is a time when we have a LOT of expectations put onto us, yet our body is hurting, our hormones are going into overdrive, and we're questioning everything we're doing. This time can also be seen as a time of loss: the loss of our previous selves and our pre-birth bodies. The transition of birth to postpartum can hit home really hard, yet society expects us to smile, bounce back, and get on with it.

I found the postpartum stage hard. I was a new mother, grieving the loss of my own mum, and facing a global lockdown. I didn't have my mum to guide me, nor did I have the support I needed. My C-section scar got infected twice, and I felt like

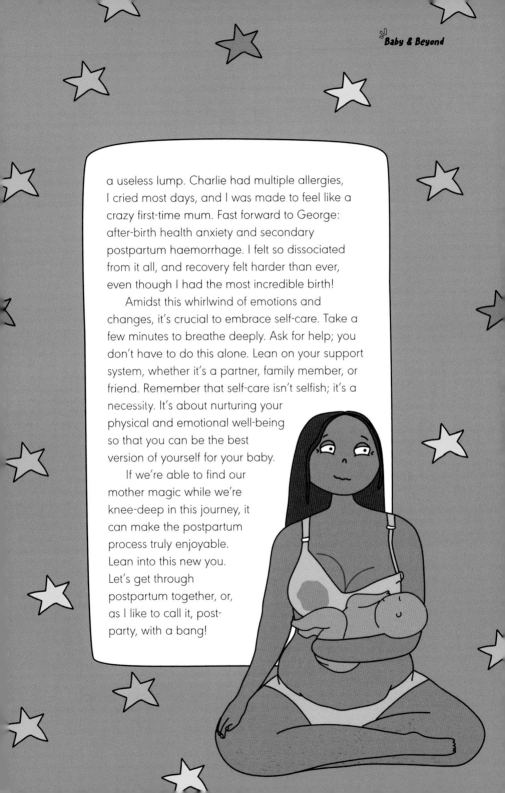

a useless lump. Charlie had multiple allergies,
I cried most days, and I was made to feel like a
crazy first-time mum. Fast forward to George:
after-birth health anxiety and secondary
postpartum haemorrhage. I felt so dissociated
from it all, and recovery felt harder than ever,
even though I had the most incredible birth!

Amidst this whirlwind of emotions and
changes, it's crucial to embrace self-care. Take a
few minutes to breathe deeply. Ask for help; you
don't have to do this alone. Lean on your support
system, whether it's a partner, family member, or
friend. Remember that self-care isn't selfish; it's a
necessity. It's about nurturing your
physical and emotional well-being
so that you can be the best
version of yourself for your baby.

If we're able to find our
mother magic while we're
knee-deep in this journey, it
can make the postpartum
process truly enjoyable.
Lean into this new you.
Let's get through
postpartum together, or,
as I like to call it, post-
party, with a bang!

Mother magic

You've just become a mum; do you know what this means? The rebirth of you and the start of a transformation into the magic of Motherhood.

You did it! Urm hello butterfly, you've been through a metamorphosis, and babe, you've gained Mother Magic. You've walked out of those flames like a queen.

While this section of the book is going to get RAW and REAL with the nitty-gritty (and sometimes shitty) parts of postpartum, it's also an opportunity to stop and think just how incredible you are. You've just brought life into the world and gone through some big changes. I know you might be looking at yourself thinking, "Why do I still look pregnant? Why does my body look like that?", but I want to remind you of the POWER of you, your creation, and self-acceptance. It's now more than ever that you may feel unlike yourself. You might miss the old you.

Or for some, grieve their bump. However you are feeling, know that there are millions of others around the world going through the exact same right now. And we are with you babe.

Take your time

These next 12 weeks are all about you and your baby. Lock the doors, postpone the visitors, snuggle in bed, and take it all in. In Western culture, precious time has been robbed of us. Hollywood strikes again! Woo-fucking-hoo. But seriously, you've done a lot of hard work. And now it's time to recover, heal, and bond with your baby.

 Use this time as an opportunity to focus on yourself, and your baby.

Don't be afraid to challenge the social norms of "bouncing back" (for example, taking pictures to put online of you walking the baby with a forced smile a few days after birth) and instead relish the fact that you get to CHILL the hell out! You can say no to visitors by kindly sending a message to everyone asking for some privacy while you settle into motherhood and get to know your baby. Use this time as an opportunity to focus on yourself, and your baby. You deserve it.

Soak it all up

While you navigate this time, make sure you've got good close support – whether that's your partner, friend, or a family member. Let them know what you need and set the expectations of this slow time to be present, heal, and for them to hold space for you.

Spend time sleeping, eating, and cuddling your newborn. Don't get hung up on the small stuff, the mess, or the fact the nursery isn't quite set up yet. Know that your baby will most likely want to be close to you, sleep on you, and cuddle you, as they don't even know they're separate from you until they're around seven months old.

Tapping into your mother magic

Yep, it's a real thing. The first thing you need to know about your mother magic is that you are absolutely perfect for your baby. You are the best mum for them and you have a connection that is completely unique. Whether you felt it instantly or are still finding your feet, it's okay, it doesn't make your magic any less.

Here are some ways to help tap into your power:

- Be kind to yourself
- Lower expectations
- Journal your feelings
- Bond with your baby
- Take time to be present
- Appreciate your body
- Listen to your intuition
- Seek out support

Post-party prep

The bit most people forget is the prep for postpartum, but what you should be thinking about when preparing for your baby is looking after YOU!

Food

It's really important to ensure you, or someone else, batch cook yourself some easy, nutritious meals and freeze them. Allow them to be accessible and just pop them in the microwave when you are hungry. It's also handy to have some snacks in to help you through longer nights. Once baby is here you need to eat, even if you don't feel like it. During this time nutrients and vitamins are going to be a massive help to your mental and physical well-being. So here are some tips on making food, including not even having to cook!

Stockpile snacks! Healthy ones are best, but don't feel bad for biting into a lovely bar of choc.

Get family and friends to set up a meal train - it's super helpful.

Keep snacks in your caddy - they'll help you through those long nights of feeding.

Batch cook yourself some easy and nutritious meals and freeze them.

Try taking some PP vitamins and probiotics to support your gut.

Invest in a slow cooker or pressure cooker so you can chuck all that good stuff in one pot, in one go.

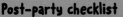

Post-party checklist

- Food prep, snacks, and drinks
- Contact numbers
- Nappies, cotton wool, and warm flask
- Changing mat, nappy bags, and rash cream
- Nursing pillow
- Big fat maternity pads
- Nipple pads
- Phone chargers and earphones
- Muslin cloths and flannels
- Blanket and tissues
- Vests for baby and change of clothes for you

Support

It's very easy to slip into an attitude of "I'll do it myself" or "I don't want to ask for help", but the truth is we may need that help. Speak to family and friends beforehand and discuss what kind of things you may need help with, including chores, food, or maybe just a cuppa. Here's a handy list you can write out and pop on your fridge. If you use a whiteboard pen you'll be able to rub off and change as and when needed.

- Please put a load in the washer
- Please help me clean
- Watch baby while I shower
- I'd love a hot cuppa
- Please bring me food
- Please help with care of my other children
- Watch baby while I sleep

Super stations

Babe, trust me when I say, shit will be everywhere. I've been in the thick of it! This is one of my favourite hacks – stations. They can be baskets or boxes or even a bag. Place them around the house to ensure you have everything you need, when you need it. You'll need at least two stations. One will be where you and baby sleep and the other will be the place where you'll spend most of your time in the day. Each station will have all baby's things and the most important stuff you need too.

- Nappies
- Nappy sacks
- Cotton pads
- Breast pads
- Nipple cream
- Vapour rub
- Nappy cream
- Muslins
- Wipes
- Baby clothes
- PJs for you
- Water bottle
- Snacks
- Charger
- List of contacts

Head-to-toe changes

What the fuck is going on in your body?

"Hot flushes"

Hormones are flying! It's like being pregnant all over again. Remember, your body has grown a baby for many months, and the comedown of getting things back to normal means some hot flushes, sweat, and continuous weeing.

"Booby traps"

Breast engorgement may result in firm and full breasts. This may feel sore and painful. Engorgement usually occurs within 24-72 hours postpartum.

"Shivering"

You may experience shivering shortly after birth, which may last a couple of minutes to an hour. Your body has been through a lot, and you can thank your hormones for this phenomenon.

"Jelly belly"

Having a shelf and loose skin is very normal at this time. It's just stretched over 9 months - you can't expect it to bounce back! You may also notice your abdominal walls have separated, but these should go back within 6-8 weeks.

"Cindy cervix"

The cervix remains dilated 2-3cm (0.7-1in) for the first few days after birth. It does not go back to the shape it was before. Instead of a smooth circular opening, it turns into a large transverse slit. It takes the cervix 3-4 months to fully recover after birth.

"Tiger stripes"

Stretchmarks change from a pink/red colour to silver. These are permanent. Chloasma and hyperpigmentation from pregnancy usually resolve themselves.

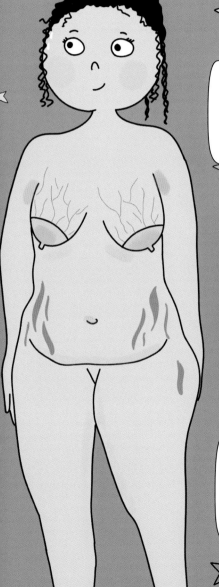

"Arghh my hair"

Hair loss may be present between 1–5 months postpartum. Usually, normal hair growth resumes by 6–15 months postpartum.

"Pain in the arse'

You may find yourself constipated, and haemorrhoids may develop due to hormonal shifts and pain medication. Don't worry – I have all the hacks for this on page 178!

"After pains"

Just when birth is over, we are faced with a contracting uterus, which is helping to shed the lining and get everything back to normal. This can be super uncomfortable but won't last forever.

"Bleeding hell"

The lining of your uterus sheds after the placenta comes out so that a new layer of tissue can regenerate. This is where the long-ass period-type bleeding comes into play, also known as lochia. You may notice it more when you breastfeed, as this contracts the uterus. Lochia can last up to 12 weeks. If you find yourself seeing large clots, speak to your care provider.

"Feeling a bit peri peri"

Your perineum is going to feel pretty tender. That may be just because it has stretched to accommodate your baby, or because you've had a graze or tear. This will heal over time.

All the firsts

You're thinking WOAH right? Let's delve deeper into these bodily changes and how we can navigate them with our mother magic, ease, and game-changing hacks!

Peri peri problems

Is your perineum feeling tender? It may be stretched out right now, or have a tear. Here are some methods for soothing that sore perineal area.

Indulge in a warm (not hot) sitz bath (a shallow bath covering the area).

Fill up a plastic bottle with warm water and spray as you wee.

Avoid standing or sitting for long periods.

Avoid heavy lifting or strenuous exercise for 4-6 weeks.

Witch hazel! Mix with water spray on a pad and stick in the fridge. Avoid freezing as if it's too cold it won't promote healing and may even hinder it.

Avoid smoking as it slows down the healing process.

Big cotton pants are a must - breathable and comfy.

Begin doing your pelvic floor exercises as soon as you can after birth. This will increase the blood supply and help with healing.

MUM STORIES

"The Floppy Face, Floppy Fanny and 'breathing baby out' techniques worked like a dream for my first postpartum poo! Techniques for life!"

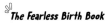

Pain in the arsehole

The first poo after birth can be a tricky one! Things are swollen, of course, and you may have haemorrhoids or a little constipation from labour.

Avoid straining as it puts pressure on your rectal area.

Drink plenty of water.

Add fibre to your diet. It helps to soften your stool while giving it more bulk. A high-fibre diet helps prevent constipation, which makes haemorrhoids worse.

Try not to use dry toilet roll – instead use fragrance-free wipes.

Get yourself a foot stool. Literally a game changer!

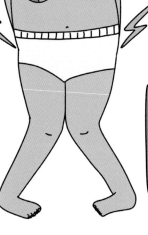

Try taking a natural stool softener.

Bring a big U-shaped pregnancy pillow for after the first poo, and smaller V-shaped ones to sit on everywhere else in the house.

Think floppy face, floppy fanny - relaxing your jaw allows your pelvic floor muscles to relax, which in turn gives your bumhole a break.

Bloody hell

Lochia (bleeding after birth) happens after every type of birth. Your uterus has been period-free for nine months and it's time to shed the lining and return to the norm.

Look out for lots of large blood clots or more than a pint of blood in 24 hours. If you notice this, tell your midwife straight away.

Bleeding is completely normal for up to six weeks after birth – think of it as a heavy period.

If in doubt, speak to someone – don't worry about making that call.

Stock up on BIG FAT maternity pads or comfy reusable ones.

Avoid tampons.

When you breastfeed, your uterus will contract (so watch out for extra blood).

Keep wipes and pads in your caddy nearby for quick changes.

It's a bitch, but it won't last forever!

Ultimate C-section aftercare

You've just been through nothing short of major abdominal surgery. This isn't something to brush off and it's important to look after yourself and your scar!

Big, baggy clothes and maternity leggings are a must. Oh, and big pants!

Keep a pillow in the car to protect your scar from the seatbelt.

Take it SLOW and EASY! You've just had major surgery.

Drink green tea and/or peppermint tea to reduce trapped wind.

Your body has been through a lot. For a reminder about self-acceptance, turn to page 16.

Air your scar as much as possible. Yep, that might mean a bit of nakedness around the house!

Use a pregnancy pillow for sleeping slightly upright, it will help with getting up in the middle of the night for feeds.

Experiment with different breastfeeding positions, like football hold or lying down.

Epsom salt baths for the win!

Keep an eye out for any signs of infection and contact your GP straight away if unsure.

Scar massages!

Start with very low impact and gentle exercise when you feel ready. Walking is the best and easiest option.

Wash your scar every day, pat dry, and use scar cream from six weeks.

Birth trauma

Navigating birth trauma is hard. It's not your fault, and it's okay to feel big emotions about your birth. There is always light in darkness, and you will get through it.

Over 45% of women experience some form of birth trauma in their lifetime. This trauma can manifest in various ways and under different circumstances. Whether it was an experience completely out of your control or the birth of your dreams didn't quite align with reality, birth trauma can leave deep emotional scars. You might find yourself feeling lost, overwhelmed, or disconnected from your body and the present moment. Perhaps you missed that precious first moment with your baby due to unforeseen circumstances. It's essential to recognise that the emotions tied to our birth stories can have a profound impact on how we show up in life.

Understanding birth trauma

Most often, birth trauma is rooted in a sense of not being heard or losing control during the birthing process. These feelings can linger, affecting your overall well-being and the way you interact with your baby and those around you.

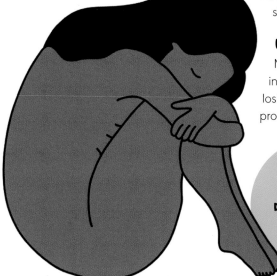

YOU MIGHT FIND YOURSELF DISCONNECTED FROM YOUR BODY AND THE PRESENT.

Acknowledge your feelings, practise self-compassion, and seek help when needed.

Techniques for managing birth trauma

1. Self-compassion: Begin by offering yourself the same compassion and love you would to your best friend. Understand that your feelings are valid and it's okay to grieve the birth experience you had envisioned.

2. Mindfulness Practise being present in the moment. Engage in mindfulness exercises to reconnect with your body and emotions. This can help you process and release the trauma.

3. Journalling Writing down your thoughts and feelings can be incredibly therapeutic. Use a journal as a safe space to express your emotions and work through them.

4. Breathing and relaxation techniques Deep-breathing exercises and relaxation techniques can help manage anxiety and stress.

Seeking help

If you find yourself struggling to cope with birth trauma, and your emotional well-being is severely impacted, it's crucial to reach out for help. Remember, there's no shame in seeking support; in fact, it's a sign of strength.

1. Talk to a therapist A trained therapist or counsellor can provide a safe space for you to explore and heal from birth trauma. They can offer guidance and coping strategies tailored to your specific needs.

2. Support groups Consider joining a support group for women who have experienced birth trauma. Sharing your feelings and hearing from others who have gone through similar experiences can be incredibly comforting.

3. Lean on loved ones Don't hesitate to lean on your loved ones for emotional support. Share your feelings and experiences with those you trust.

Healing from birth trauma is a journey that requires compassion, patience, and sometimes, professional support. By acknowledging your feelings, practising self-compassion, and seeking help when needed, you can reclaim your strength and resilience. Remember, you're not alone.

"It's an emotional rollercoaster. I found that lowering my expectations and using breathwork really helped me to manage the sensations."

Hormones and emotions

What goes up, must come down. Here's what to expect when those elevated hormone levels crash after birth.

The birth of your sweet bundle of joy is undoubtedly one of the most exciting moments of your life. No matter how long you labour or what time you give birth — yes, even if it's at 3 a.m. — you'll likely feel an amazing, indescribable high when you meet your baby for the first time, or shortly thereafter. But those surging hormones will plummet over the next few days. Here's what's going on:

> **Progesterone and oestrogen** decrease as soon as baby and the placenta are born.

> **Oxytocin** surges immediately following birth to compensate for the initial drops in progesterone and oestrogen. This hormone is responsible for that strong mothering instinct, but you may still experience "baby blues" within the coming weeks due to a gradual drop in oxytocin.

> **Prolactin** increases to encourage breast milk production (read more about breastfeeding on page 200).

Over the next few weeks you're going to notice a lot of high emotions, lack of sleep, and adrenaline running through your veins, and when you hit the six-week mark, the post-birth positive hormones begin to fade. This may have an impact on how you feel. Keep an eye on these feelings and seek support if needed.

Look out for... Around the six-week mark, symptoms of postpartum depression may begin to show, as those positive post-birth hormones continue to fade. The changes you should look for closely are: not wanting to shower or focus on hygiene; being afraid of leaving your baby with someone else; not being able to sleep fully due to continually checking on baby; and a lack of desire for common tasks.

Post-hormone hacks

Balanced nutrition Eating is essential for keeping your hormones regulated. Choose foods that are rich in nutrients and those supporting balance like Omega-3 fatty acids, found in fish and flaxseeds.

Stay hydrated Proper hydration is key for hormonal balance – drink plenty of water to support your body's natural functions.

Gentle exercise While cosying up with baby in those early weeks make sure you still regularly move your body.

Supplements Think about a PP supplement, or take your placenta pills to help balance your hormones and mood.

Keep an eye out for postpartum depression at around six weeks.

Remind yourself what all these hormones are about on page 75.

Celebrating wins

Being a new mum is hard. Lower your expectations, and let's start celebrating those wins! Tick as you go. You're fucking awesome!

- [ ] I showered today - woohoo
- [ ] I got dressed
- [ ] First walk around a local park
- [ ] First trip out
- [ ] First car journey
- [ ] I breastfed in public
- [ ] I played with my baby
- [ ] I allowed myself to feel good
- [ ] I managed to drink a hot tea
- [ ] I visited my first mum-and-baby group
- [ ] I met up with a friend
- [ ] I reached out for help
- [ ] I didn't put pressure on myself
- [ ] I wrote down some wins

It's normal to feel anxious or worried and to suffer with baby blues. Think back to your prep for birth and use the skills you learnt in breathwork. It's a very powerful tool that can give you what you need to instil calm in just a moment. If things get overwhelming, leave baby in a safe space and step out to take a deep breath. If you are thinking about harming yourself or your baby, or if you are concerned about someone, call a mental health helpline now. Or get someone you trust to help you make the call.

Tip: *Every night before you go to bed, write a little list of all your "wins" that day. This will help you keep positive and fight off postpartum blues.*

Mother and baby connection

Creating connections and building a secure attachment with your baby will be beneficial for both you and your baby's brain development.

Bonding after birth

The connection between a mother and her baby is a profound and beautiful journey that begins the moment that tiny heartbeat is detected. However, it doesn't end with birth. In fact, it's just the beginning. Let's explore the various aspects of nurturing a secure

attachment, through small but meaningful activities The truth is, not everyone feels that love-at-first-sight moment that is often portrayed as the norm. Either way, it's okay. Sometimes you need time. I felt love instantly with Charlie but with George it felt like a bit of a blur. I didn't feel the same excitement and joy, and it wasn't until a few weeks later that it clicked into place.

Connections that matter

Building a strong bond is not solely about meeting your baby's physical needs but also about emotional connection. Responding to your baby's cues promptly and consistently creates a sense of security. Your baby learns that their needs will be met, fostering trust in the relationship.

Bonding through babywearing

Carrying your baby close to your heart through babywearing is an age-old practice that continues to be invaluable. It provides comfort and security for your little one, while also allowing you to go about your daily activities. Whether using a sling, wrap, or carrier, babywearing enhances your bond by keeping your baby close and engaged with the world through your perspective. Not only is it a lifesaver when it comes to being hands-free but it comes with so many benefits. Here is my guide so you can enjoy it just as much as I did.

Nurture a secure attachment through small but meaningful bonding activities.

Benefits of babywearing
- May help avoid spinal and cranial deformities
- Prevents flat head syndrome
- Supports breastfeeding
- Babies are more able to regulate their own physiological functions (breathing, heart rate, temperature)
- Gives you two free arms

Tips
- Use soft, structured carriers
- Baby's airway should be clear
- Check your carrier for signs of wear or damage periodically
- Baby should stay in an upright position

Pulling fabric up to baby's knees creates a seat for them, and helps with proper hip alignment.

Baby's hips are not aligned properly. This positioning can increase force on the hip joint, which can lead to hip dysplasia.

Activities that strengthen bonds

1. Massage Gentle baby massage not only relaxes your baby but also strengthens your physical connection. It's an excellent way to spend quality time together while promoting relaxation and bonding.

2. Reading Reading to your baby, even from a very young age, is a beautiful way to introduce them to the world of words and storytelling. It also provides a soothing and bonding experience.

3. Singing and talking Your voice is a source of comfort for your baby. Singing lullabies, or simply talking to your baby as you go about your day, helps them become familiar with your voice and strengthens your emotional connection.

4. Playtime Age-appropriate playtime activities, such as peek-a-boo, tummy time, or playing with soft toys, not only aid in your baby's development but also deepen your bond through shared experiences.

How to create a secure attachment

Creating a secure attachment is an ongoing process that involves love, patience, and consistency. Here are some tips:

- **Be responsive** Respond to your baby's needs promptly and with empathy. This helps them feel safe and understood.

- **Trust your instincts** As a parent, you know your baby better than anyone. Trust your instincts and build your unique bond.

- **Self-care** Remember to take care of yourself. A rested and emotionally well-balanced parent can better meet their baby's needs.

The small things that matter

It's the little gestures that often have the most significant impact. Smiles, cuddles, and maintaining eye contact during feeding or nappy changes all contribute to creating a loving and secure environment for your baby.

The journey of motherhood is filled with love, joy, and connection. By focusing on bonding, connections, engaging activities, and small but meaningful gestures, you are creating a foundation of love and security that will guide your child's development and strengthen your bond for years to come. Cherish every moment of this remarkable journey.

A "good" baby

The "good baby" narrative is a societal problem and one which can put immense pressure on what babies should be like.

Okay, let's chat about the infamous myth of the "good baby". This phrase is like nails on a chalkboard for me. It really gets my feathers ruffled, and you know what? It's a myth that seems to pop up everywhere! But here's the real deal: there's no such thing as a "bad", "naughty", or a "manipulative" baby. Nope, not a chance! Babies are little bundles of innocence and purity, incapable of controlling you in such ways.

When a baby cries, moans, or makes any kind of noise, they're sending us a signal, a message that needs our attention. Take sleep, for instance. Imagine expecting a baby to snooze through the night without needing a little drink or comfort. I mean,

when was the last time you managed to sleep a solid 12 hours without tossing, turning, or reaching for a sip of water? It's pretty rare, right?

Trust me on this, every baby is as unique as a snowflake, and their actions are shaped by a myriad of factors. Their birth experience, their individual needs, and the environment they're in all play a part in who they are and how they express themselves. So, let's ditch the "good baby" myth and embrace the beautiful, wonderfully unique babies in our lives!

REMINDER

Don't get lost in the opinions of shoulds and musts, and instead go with the flow of your baby's needs - you'll feel more connected.

Newborn hacks

Having a newborn can be confusing, conflicting, and just a bit mind-boggling. That's why you need some hacks for understanding them! These are my absolute faves.

Feeding baby

It's normal for your baby to have different needs when it comes to feeding. Sticking to a schedule of three hours between feeds can cause issues for some. Feeding on demand takes into the notion that your baby is growing, changing, and has their unique needs. At the start this can be hard, as there will be a lot of change, cluster feeding, and an up-and-down routine. However, they'll slowly start to find a way that works for them.

Tip: *Try to avoid using a dummy/ pacifier when your baby is first born as this can confuse and inhibit natural feeding cues. Instead, use after six weeks. If earlier, ensure baby has fed beforehand.*

HUNGER CUES

Here's some signs your baby may be giving you.

Early cues (I'm getting hungry)

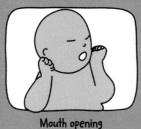

Stirring   Mouth opening   Turning head seeking/routing

Mid cues (I'm really hungry)

Stretching   Increased physical movement   Hand to mouth

Late cues (Calm me and feed me ASAP)

Crying   Agitated movements   Turning red

To calm your baby, try: · Skin-to-skin on chest · Cuddling · Talking · Stroking · Sshhing

NEWBORN POOS

Green/black (sticky, tar-like)
This is normal for your baby's first poo. It's called meconium and will change in the first couple of days.

Mustard yellow
For a breastfed baby, this is normal. It will be loose and a bit runny.

Darker yellow
Formula-fed babies tend to have darker and slightly firmer poo.

Frothy green
Can happen with babies breastfed from both breasts frequently. Try feeding until one breast is drained before switching. It can also be a sign of an allergy.

Dark green
Sometimes found with babies on formula, because of the iron found in the formula. It's usually nothing to worry about.

Green/brown
As you start to introduce solid food, this will be one of the many shades you can expect to see in your baby's nappy.

Orange
Another example of the variety of colours solid foods can produce in your baby's poo.

Brown
As they get older, your baby's poo will be more like grown-up poo.

If you notice any of the following types of poo in a nappy, see your doctor and take a nappy with you.

Red Blood in poo could be from constipation, if mum has bleeding nipples, or something more serious. If your baby is female then it could also be "false menses" as the maternal hormones leave the baby's system.

Chalk white White or grey poo is not normal and could be a sign of a liver problem.

Black Baby poo should only be green or black during the first few days; after that it could be a sign of something more serious.

How to change a nappy

1. Gather supplies Have a clean nappy, wipes, and a changing mat ready.

2. Prepare the area Lay your baby on the changing mat or a clean, flat surface.

3. Safety first Keep one hand on your baby at all times to prevent rolling.

4. Open the old nappy Use wipes for a first, gentle clean of baby's bottom, then fold up the nappy.

5. Lift legs Lift your baby's legs gently by the ankles to slide out the dirty nappy.

6. Clean baby Use wipes to clean your baby's bottom gently but well, wiping from front to back.

7. Place the clean nappy Slide the clean nappy under your baby, with tabs at the back.

8. Fasten securely Bring the front of the nappy up and secure the tabs snugly.

9. Dispose of waste Making sure baby is secure on the table, dispose of the dirty nappy and wipes properly.

10. Wash hands: Wash your hands thoroughly.

Nappy hacks

Colour indicator Not sure if it's time for a change? The colour-changing wetness indicator line on many nappies is your go-to guide.

Size up If you're dealing with constant leaks, try sizing up. That extra space could be just what you need to prevent messes.

Front-to-back Always wipe from front to back to prevent infections, especially with baby girls.

Stock up Keep a mini stockpile of nappies, wipes, and cream in every room you frequently use. It saves you from running around!

Gentle clean Baby wipes are handy, but a warm, wet cloth can be gentler on the skin, reducing chances of nappy rash.

REMINDER

Practice makes perfect, and you'll get quicker with each nappy change.

NEWBORN SLEEP

First of all, anyone who tells you newborns should sleep through the night clearly own unicorns or are pretty uneducated on the circadian rhythms of us humans! Just like us, babies will wake for a number of reasons including hunger, thirst, toilet, or comfort.

For a secure attachment, babies like to be close to their mums. Avoid putting baby in a different room for at least six months or even a year. Maybe not even then if you're happy bed-sharing.

Tip: *Always follow safer sleep guidelines via the Lullaby Trust.*

The magic of newborn sleep

Babies are amazing little sleepers, but they come with their own set of rules. Remember, every baby is unique, so what works for one might not work for another. Let's dive into some newborn sleep basics!

Generalised wake windows (up to 12 weeks)

0–2 weeks: Your newborn will snooze for most of the day, waking up every two to three hours for feeds.

2–6 weeks: You might start to notice slightly longer awake periods between naps, but still, expect several short naps during the day and night. Hang in there; this is normal!

6–12 weeks: Some babies begin to develop a routine. They might stay awake for about 45 minutes to 1½ hours between naps.

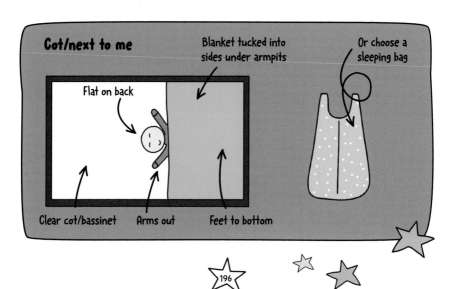

Cot/next to me

Blanket tucked into sides under armpits

Or choose a sleeping bag

Flat on back

Clear cot/bassinet   Arms out   Feet to bottom

Embrace the regressions

Around the four-month mark, many babies experience sleep regressions. It's a plot twist! During these times, they might wake up more frequently or have trouble falling asleep. But don't worry – it's an amazing sign of growth and development.

Tips for peaceful sleep

1. Create a cosy sleep environment A dark, quiet, and comfortably cool room is ideal. White noise is also your ally.

2. Swaddle or sleep sacks Some babies love to feel snug as a bug in a swaddle, while others prefer the freedom of sleep sacks.

3. Follow their cues Pay attention to your baby's sleepy signals. Yawning, rubbing eyes, and fussiness are all signs that it's naptime.

4. Establish a calming bedtime routine A soothing bath, a lullaby, or a gentle book can signal to your baby that it's time to wind down.

5. Share the load Ask for help from friends, family, or a partner. A well-rested parent is a happy parent.

REMINDER
Your little one's sleep patterns will evolve. Embrace the journey, share stories with fellow parents, and know that you're doing an incredible job.

If you choose to co-sleep/ bed-share with your baby:

- Avoid letting pets or other children in the bed.
- Always lay baby on their back and never leave them unattended.
- Make sure baby won't fall out of bed or get trapped between the mattress and the wall.
- Do not co-sleep on a sofa or chair.
- Keep pillows, sheets, and blankets away from your baby.
- Avoid bed-sharing if you've been drinking or smoking.

KEEPING CLEAN AND FINDING ROUTINE

It's easy to get worried about establishing routines in the early days. The odd comment from a friend or family member of "well I always..." can send you into overdrive. Remember: you know best for your baby and while some routine might be helpful, it often changes a lot during the newborn phase!

Baby's umbilical cord

Your baby's cord may look weird as it starts to dry up over the coming days or weeks. It will fall away naturally, but keeping it dry and clean is essential. My favourite way to do this is using colostrum, breast milk, and a cotton bud. Lift around the cord, apply the milk or clean water. Air-dry, and then tuck in the nappy for less irritation.

The first bath

Try to postpone baby's bath for at least a week. Remember that gorgeous vernix we spoke about and

Newborns are constantly changing, growing, and needing different things.

all that good bacteria! Over this first week or so, the good bacteria is colonising and protecting your baby. When you decide bath time has come, make sure to just use warm water, no products, and soft cotton pads to get in any creases. Avoid bathing baby every day so as not to dry their skin out, and continue to use water and cotton pads to get to the hard-to-reach areas like armpits and under the neck. They can get sore if not regularly checked and again, air dry or use a cotton pad.

Drop expectations

Routine can be a beautiful thing and works really well for some, especially in the early weeks. However, newborns are constantly changing, growing and needing different things at different times, so if your routine gets thrown out the window, instead of hitting a brick wall, embrace the chaos and move with your baby's needs. Don't worry about it and trust that this too shall pass.

SUPERVISE YOUR BABY AT ALL TIMES

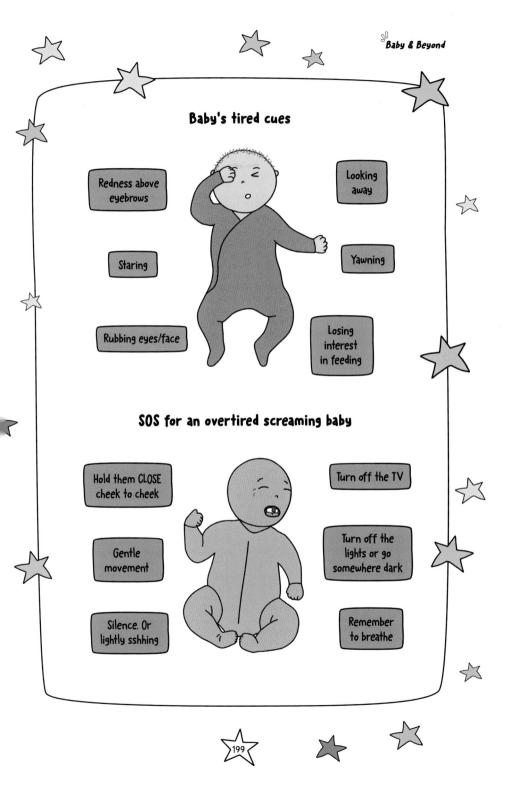

Baby's tired cues

Redness above eyebrows

Looking away

Staring

Yawning

Rubbing eyes/face

Losing interest in feeding

SOS for an overtired screaming baby

Hold them CLOSE cheek to cheek

Turn off the TV

Gentle movement

Turn off the lights or go somewhere dark

Silence. Or lightly sshhing

Remember to breathe

Breastfeeding

Breastfeeding has so many benefits, but it's not always easy or possible to achieve. Let's look at how you can do it.

Breastfeeding is more than just nourishment. It's a beautiful way to provide for and bond with your precious newborn. It's a journey filled with incredible benefits, not only for your little one but for you too. From offering complex immunity through live breast milk to reducing your risk of high blood pressure, diabetes, and even certain cancers, breastfeeding is a gift to both mother and baby. I breastfed my first for two and a half years and am currently breastfeeding my second, six months in at the time of writing this book.

Both journeys have been difficult for me but I wouldn't change them for the world. I feel so lucky and proud that I had the opportunity to continue to breastfeed. This doesn't mean it's for everyone, but it comes with a hell of a lot of benefits and very few cons. Plus, it's an eco-friendly choice that saves money and reduces waste, and, let's face it, it's super convenient when your little one needs a quick snack!

Breastfeeding challenges

However, the path of breastfeeding can be challenging. Many mothers find themselves facing hurdles, from pain to the mysteries of milk production, often leading to a decline in breastfeeding after just a few weeks. Let's delve deep into the nitty-gritty of breastfeeding and provide you with the wisdom and support you

BREASTMILK CONTAINS 200 DIFFERENT SUBSTANCES AND CHANGES DAILY TO SUIT YOUR BABY'S NEEDS.

 Your baby's saliva is like a secret language sending signals back through your nipples.

need to make an informed choice. Whether you're a first-time mum or looking for a fresh start, let's uncover the secrets and support you in your breastfeeding journey. It's time to embrace the beauty and benefits of breastfeeding with confidence!

Breast milk and baby

Newborn growth charts can be extremely daunting, so try not to worry – remember that the best way to give baby more is by allowing them to be on the breast more. Feed on demand. This allows your boobs to make more milk. It is possible to exclusively breastfeed your baby. Combined feeding by topping up with formula will lower your supply, seek out the right support before choosing this option, and make a decision that feels good for you.

Newborn stomach capacity

It's normal for some babies to lose weight after they've been born. It's also normal for you to produce only the tiniest amounts of milk. Use your instincts when discussing this to ensure you don't fall into a narrative of being told you're not giving them enough. If you ever worry about this, I highly recommend a lactation consultant who is extremely experienced in breastfeeding. Reminder, more boob time = more boob milk!

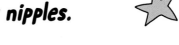

Day 1	**Day 3**
1–1.5 teaspoons	20–30ml (0.75–1oz)

1 week	**1 month**
40–60ml (1.5–2oz)	70–140ml 2.5–5oz

Getting a good latch

This whole latching business can feel like a high-stakes game of Tetris! So how do we get baby to latch on and get feeding?

While latching is crucial for effective breastfeeding, it's not the end of the world if it doesn't happen straight away. You don't have to throw in the towel! Consider alternative routes like temporary nipple shields as you work on mastering the latch.

Tongue tie

If your baby can't get a deep enough latch and you are in pain, with blistered or bleeding nipples, it may be a tongue tie – a restriction of the tongue's range of motion. It is easy to sort, so speak with your care provider for help.

Latch-friendly environment

Create a calm environment. Recline on pillows or create another kind of comfortable area. Hold your baby, preferably skin-to-skin against your bare chest. Let your baby lead. Support your baby, but don't force the latch. Allow your breast to hang naturally.

Nipple shields

Alright, let's debunk some myths and spill some truth about nipple shields. These little silicone wonders often get a bad rap, seen as a last resort or even a breastfeeding no-go. But nipple shields are total game-changers, potentially saving your breastfeeding journey when the going gets tough. The ultimate goal is for your baby to latch directly onto the breast. Using a nipple shield for a bit doesn't mean

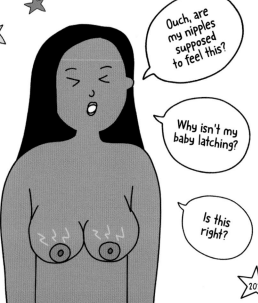

202

HOW TO GET A GOOD LATCH

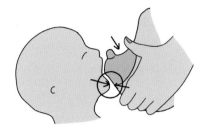

Nipple towards baby's nose, stimulating the top lip until their mouth opens wide.

Find a comfortable position. Support your breast with your other hand to ensure baby is close enough to get to your areola.

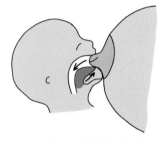

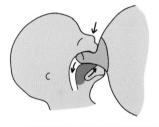

Baby's chin makes contact with breast, latching deeper below the nipple.

Baby's lip to be level and firmly against your areola. Ensure nostrils are clear for breathing. Allow baby's head to move freely.

they won't get there! They're a stepping stone: babies often transition smoothly to latching without them.

To use a nipple shield, simply place it snugly over your nipple before a feed and then let your baby latch onto the shield as they would your breast. Remember to get support for latching issues first before opting straight for this.

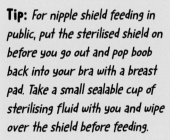

Tip: *For nipple shield feeding in public, put the sterilised shield on before you go out and pop boob back into your bra with a breast pad. Take a small sealable cup of sterilising fluid with you and wipe over the shield before feeding.*

Practically perfect pumping

Whether you're going back to work, need a break, or want to involve other caregivers, pumping can be a fantastic option. Here are some sanity-saving tips to help you master this new adventure.

Choose the right pump

If you're going to be pumping often, an electric double pump can save you time. However, if you'll only be pumping occasionally, a manual pump or even a single electric pump might do the trick. If you're unable to get milk this way, look at hand expressing. For some, this is the only way to express milk.

Get comfy

Find a quiet, comfortable space. Stress can inhibit milk flow, so maybe put on some calming music or have a picture of your baby nearby to help stimulate the let-down reflex.

Tip: *Nursing pillows provide essential support, elevating your baby to the right height and angle for breastfeeding. They alleviate the strain on your arms and shoulders, making those long nursing sessions much more comfortable.*

Timing is everything

Try to pump around the same time your baby usually feeds, to keep up with their schedule and maintain your milk supply. If your baby feeds every 3-4 hours, aim to pump every 3-4 hours.

Perfect your flange fit

The flange is the funnel-shaped piece of the breast pump that fits over your breast. A wrong-sized flange can lead to discomfort and less efficient pumping. Make sure you find the right fit – most pumps come with different size options.

Hands-on pumping

After you've started pumping, use your hands to massage your breasts, moving towards the nipple. This hands-on approach can help you express more milk, more quickly.

Don't stress over numbers

Don't get too caught up on the amount of milk you're pumping. It can vary throughout the day and even from session to session. The most important thing is that your baby is fed and happy.

Store smart

Learn how to store your breast milk safely. Freshly pumped milk can stay at room temperature for up to four hours, in the fridge for up to four days, and in the freezer for about six months. Use airtight containers and label them with the date.

Keep it clean

Always remember to thoroughly clean all parts that come into contact with your breast milk. You don't want any nasty bacteria contaminating that liquid gold!

Haakaa pump

A perfect way to collect breast milk from the opposite boob while breastfeeding! Suction onto your boob and watch it flow.

Formula and bottle feeding

If you're choosing formula or introducing a bottle, it's important to know your options and how to make it the best possible experience for you and your baby.

Formula feeding is a great option for those who are unable, or don't want, to breastfeed. However, formula doesn't have the same effects as breast milk as it isn't a live substance. Choosing the right formula for you is therefore imperative to kickstarting your baby's life journey.

Choosing the right formula

Whether you opt for a cow's milk-based formula, a hypoallergenic one, or any other specialised formula, consulting with your paediatrician can help you make an informed decision. While formula is the best option for some mums, it doesn't have the same gut-healing effect as breast milk. So what can we do to make up for it? Here's how to choose formula so that you can add and help your baby's growing body and healthy bacteria.

- Choose a formula that contains added DHA and ARA.
- Choose a formula that contains both probiotics and prebiotic fibre, or you can mix some into the formula yourself.
- Choose an organic formula if possible and pay attention to the amount of added sugar; the less sugar, the better!

Formula feeding

- Prepare the formula.
- Wash your hands and choose a bottle and teat that have been sterilised.
- Use boiled water.
- Always use the recommended ratios of formula to water and make sure to stir not shake!
- Check the temperature of the bottle before feeding to your baby.

The importance of colostrum

If you're able to provide your baby with colostrum in the initial days, that's fantastic! Colostrum, often referred to as "liquid gold", is the first milk your body produces after childbirth. It's packed with antibodies and nutrients that help protect your baby and line their gut. Even if you plan to use formula, those early doses of colostrum are a precious gift for your baby's well-being.

In the end, whether you choose to exclusively formula feed, combine with breastfeeding, or transition at some point from breastfeeding to formula, the most important thing is that your baby is nourished, loved, and thriving. Each feeding journey is unique, and what matters most is the health and happiness of you and your babe!

Paced Bottle Feeding

Paced Bottle Feeding is a way to feed that allows your baby to control the pace. It slows down the milk flow into the nipple of the bottle and the mouth, allowing the baby to suckle more slowly and take breaks when needed. It replicates how the baby would feed on the breast.

- Sit baby in an upright position.
- Go skin-to-skin for better attachment and bonding.
- Give the bottle on a parallel.
- Allow baby to latch to the nipple of the bottle. Don't force it.
- After 20–30 seconds of feeding, tip the bottle downwards or remove it from baby's mouth to stop the flow of milk (creating a similar pattern as in breastfeeding).

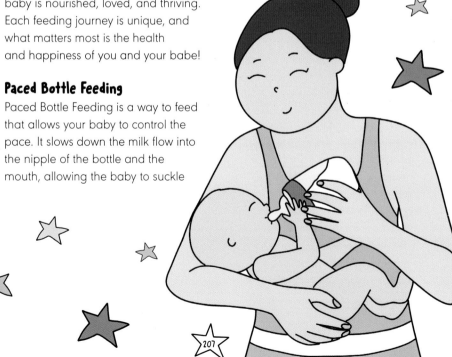

207

Colic and caveats

Colic is a popular word used a lot around newborns, but what does it mean and what can you do about it?

Even now, it's still very standard practice to be told, "oh your baby has colic... deal with it." Colic is actually a symptom of something underlying. In newborns it typically presents as episodes of excessive crying and fussiness, often occurring in the late afternoon or evening.

Signs of colic

1. Intense crying Babies with colic often cry for extended periods, sometimes for three hours or more per day, multiple days a week.

2. Predictable timing Colic episodes often follow a consistent pattern, with crying bouts occurring around the same time each day.

3. Clenched fists and arching back During episodes of colic, infants may clench their fists, arch their backs, and have tense abdominal muscles.

4. Difficulty soothing Colicky babies can be challenging to comfort, and typical soothing techniques may not work effectively.

5. No clear reason The crying doesn't appear to be related to hunger, nappy changes, or other obvious causes. It can be frustrating for both the baby and caregivers.

Not only is this clearly stressful for the baby but my gosh it can send any new mum into anxiety overdrive! If just left alone, as usually recommended, colic tends to improve by the time a baby reaches three to four months of age. However, colic is usually a manifestation of various underlying issues or conditions. Here are some potential underlying problems that could cause colic-like symptoms in your newborn.

 Colic is usually a manifestation of underlying issues or conditions.

1. Food allergies or sensitivities

Some babies may have allergies or sensitivities to components in breast milk or formula, such as cow's milk protein or soy. This can lead to gastrointestinal discomfort and excessive crying. Our bodies are not designed to process dairy, which is why some babies find it difficult to digest.

2. Gastroesophageal reflux (GERD)

Infants with GERD may experience pain and discomfort due to stomach acid flowing back into the oesophagus. This can lead to irritability and crying, which can be mistaken for colic.

3. Lactose intolerance

A lactose-intolerant baby may have difficulty digesting lactose, a sugar found in milk. This can result in gas, bloating, and fussiness.

4. Digestive immaturity

Some infants may have underdeveloped digestive systems, which can make them more prone to discomfort after feeding.

5. Overstimulation or sensory sensitivities

Some babies may be more sensitive to environmental stimuli, which can lead to overstimulation. Creating a calm and soothing environment can help alleviate these symptoms.

6. Maternal diet

In breastfeeding babies, the mother's diet can play a role. Certain foods or substances might affect the baby if they are passed through breast milk.

7. Family history

There might be a genetic component to colic, so a family history of colic or gastrointestinal issues could be a factor.

It's important to trust your instincts and speak out if you're concerned about colic. Work with your care provider to address the specific underlying cause of your baby's colic-like symptoms. This may involve dietary changes (for the baby or breastfeeding mother), help for reflux, or other approaches tailored to the individual infant's needs. This holistic approach to understanding and addressing colic can lead to better outcomes for both the baby and you!

BABY & BEYOND
Key points

Mother magic

You are transformed and you did it! Take this time to rest, bond with your baby, and allow yourself to recover and heal. You have the right to say no to visitors, cuddle up in bed, and take your sweet-ass time during these beautiful first weeks.

MUM

Newborn hacks

Now you've got a newborn, you may be thinking, what do i do now? Literally no one knows how to change a nappy or what to look out for when they first become a mum. Tapping into instincts is important, but having the hacks can definitely make life easier and less anxious. You know your baby better than anyone else; use this as a guide to create your own confidence.

Head-to-toe changes

The beauty of birth also comes with a lot of bodily and emotional changes. Hormones are flying. You may notice afterpains, hair loss, and bleeding to name a few, but it's all part of the process. You've just grown a whole human! Follow the tips and be kind to yourself.

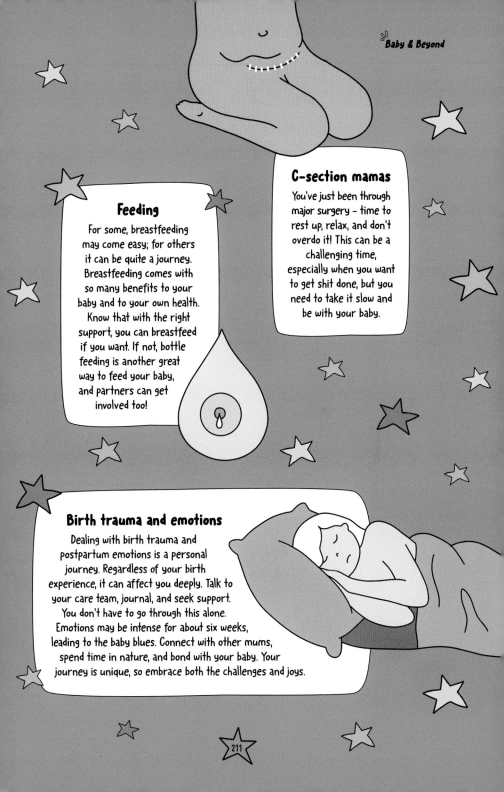

Feeding

For some, breastfeeding may come easy; for others it can be quite a journey. Breastfeeding comes with so many benefits to your baby and to your own health. Know that with the right support, you can breastfeed if you want. If not, bottle feeding is another great way to feed your baby, and partners can get involved too!

C-section mamas

You've just been through major surgery – time to rest up, relax, and don't overdo it! This can be a challenging time, especially when you want to get shit done, but you need to take it slow and be with your baby.

Birth trauma and emotions

Dealing with birth trauma and postpartum emotions is a personal journey. Regardless of your birth experience, it can affect you deeply. Talk to your care team, journal, and seek support. You don't have to go through this alone. Emotions may be intense for about six weeks, leading to the baby blues. Connect with other mums, spend time in nature, and bond with your baby. Your journey is unique, so embrace both the challenges and joys.

211

Bibliography

p.19 Bremner JD. Traumatic stress: effects on the brain. Dialogues Clin Neurosci. 2006 Dec. https://www.ncbi.nlm.nih.gov/pmc/articles/PMC3181836/

p.19 Kim EJ, Pellman B, Kim JJ. Stress effects on the hippocampus: a critical review. Learning and Memory. 2015, Aug. https://www.ncbi.nlm.nih.gov/pmc/articles/PMC4561403/

p.24 Hevesi K, Horvath Z, Sal D, Miklos E, Rowland DL. Faking orgasm: relationship to orgasmic problems and relationship type in heterosexual women. Sexual Medicine. 2021 Oct. https://www.ncbi.nlm.nih.gov/pmc/articles/PMC8498965/

p.24 Wigert H, Nilsson C, Dencker A, Begley C, Jangsten E, Sparud-Lundin C, Mollberg M, Patel H. Women's experiences of fear of childbirth: a metasynthesis of qualitative studies. Int J Qual Stud Health Well-being. 2020 Dec. https://www.ncbi.nlm.nih.gov/pmc/articles/PMC6968519/

p.28 Uddin LQ, Nomi JS, Hébert-Seropian B, Ghaziri J, Boucher O. Structure and function of the human insula. J Clin Neurophysiol. 2017 Jul.

https://www.ncbi.nlm.nih.gov/pmc/articles/PMC6032992/

p.29 Rubin Rachael D, Watson Patrick D, Duff Melissa C, Cohen Neal J. The role of the hippocampus in flexible cognition and social behavior. Frontiers in Human Neuroscience. 2014 Sept. https://www.frontiersin.org/articles/10.3389/fnhum.2014.00742/full

p.29 Scatliffe N, Casavant S, Vittner D, Cong X. Oxytocin and early parent-infant interactions: a systematic review. Int J Nurs Sci. 2019 Sept.

https://www.ncbi.nlm.nih.gov/pmc/articles/PMC6838998/

p.29 Cerritelli F, Frasch MG, Antonelli MC, Viglione C, Vecchi S, Chiera M, Manzotti A. A review on the vagusnerve and autonomic nervous system during fetal development:

searching for critical windows. Front Neurosci. 2021 Sep. https://www.ncbi.nlm.nih.gov/pmc/articles/PMC8488382/

p.30 Ahmad AH, Abdul Aziz CB. The brain in pain. Malays J Med Sci. 2014 Dec. https://www.ncbi.nlm.nih.gov/pmc/articles/PMC4405805/

p.31 Rúger-Navarrete A, Vázquez-Lara JM, Antúnez-Calvente I, Rodríguez-Díaz L, Riesco-González FJ, Palomo-Gómez R, Gómez-Salgado J, Fernández-Carrasco FJ. Antenatal fear of childbirth as a risk factor for a bad childbirth experience. Healthcare (Basel). 2023 Jan. https://www.ncbi.nlm.nih.gov/pmc/articles/PMC9914781/

p.32–33 Jepma, M, Koban, L, van Doorn, J et al. Behavioural and neural evidence for self-reinforcing expectancy effects on pain. Nat Hum Behav. 2018 Oct. https://www.nature.com/articles/s41562-018-0455-8

p.33 Olza I, Leahy-Warren P, Benyamini Y, Kazmierczak M, Karlsdottir SI, Spyridou A, Crespo-Mirasol E, Takács L, Hall PJ, Murphy M, Jonsdottir SS, Downe S, Nieuwenhuijze MJ. Women's psychological experiences of physiological childbirth: a meta-synthesis. BMJ Open. 2018 Oct. https://www.ncbi.nlm.nih.gov/pmc/articles/PMC6196808/

p.33 Çalik, KY, Karabulutlu, Ö & Yavuz, C. First do no harm – interventions during labour and maternal satisfaction: a descriptive cross-sectional study. BMC Pregnancy Childbirth. 2018 Oct. https://bmcpregnancychildbirth.biomedcentral.com/articles/10.1186/s12884-018-2054-0

p.33 Nancy K Lowe. Maternal confidence in coping with labour: A self-efficacy concept. Journal of Obstetric, Gynecologic & Neonatal Nursing, Volume 20, Issue 6, 1991. https://www.sciencedirect.com/science/article/abs/pii/S0884217515329427

p.33 Sobczak A, Taylor L, Solomon S, Ho J, Kemper S, Phillips B, Jacobson K, Castellano C,

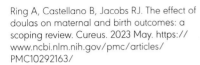

Ring A, Castellano B, Jacobs RJ. The effect of doulas on maternal and birth outcomes: a scoping review. Cureus. 2023 May. https://www.ncbi.nlm.nih.gov/pmc/articles/PMC10292163/

p.33 Deherder E, Delbaere I, Macedo A, Nieuwenhuijze MJ, Van Laere S, Beeckman K. Women's view on shared decision making and autonomy in childbirth: cohort study of Belgian women. BMC Pregnancy Childbirth. 2022 July.

https://www.ncbi.nlm.nih.gov/pmc/articles/PMC9264300/

p.33 Ondeck M. Healthy birth practice #2: walk, move around, and change positions throughout labour. J Perinat Educ. 2014 Fall. https://www.ncbi.nlm.nih.gov/pmc/articles/PMC4235058/

p.33 Smith CA, Levett KM, Collins CT, Armour M, Dahlen HG, Suganuma M. Relaxation techniques for pain management in labour. Cochrane Database Syst Rev. 2018 Mar. https://www.ncbi.nlm.nih.gov/pmc/articles/PMC6494625/

p.34 https://markandrealexander.com/2015/08/03/the-secret-of-the-reticular-activating-system/

p.35 https://www.verywellmind.com/what-is-a-confirmation-bias-2795024

p.35 https://www.webmd.com/balance/what-is-confirmation-bias

p.36 Hermann A, Bieber A, Keck T, Vaitl D, Stark R. Brain structural basis of cognitive reappraisal and expressive suppression. Soc Cogn Affect Neurosci. 2014 Sep. https://www.ncbi.nlm.nih.gov/pmc/articles/PMC4158380/

p.36 https://www.sciencedirect.com/topics/psychology/cognitive-reappraisal

p.38 https://www.ncbi.nlm.nih.gov/pmc/articles/PMC2265099/

p.48 Mendelson CR, Montalbano AP, Gao L. Fetal-to-maternal signaling in the timing of birth. J Steroid Biochem Mol Biol. 2017 Jun.

https://www.ncbi.nlm.nih.gov/pmc/articles/PMC5346347/

p.48 https://www.sciencedaily.com/releases/2004/03/040323070708.htm

p.48 https://nationalpartnership.org/wp-content/uploads/2023/02/hormonal-physiology-of-childbearing.pdf

p.49 Sprouse-Blum AS, Smith G, Sugai D, Parsa FD. Understanding endorphins and their importance in pain management. Hawaii Med J. 2010 Mar. https://www.ncbi.nlm.nih.gov/pmc/articles/PMC3104618

p.51 Swingler MM, Perry NB, Calkins SD, Bell MA. Maternal behaviour predicts infant neurophysiological and behavioural attention processes in the first year. Dev Psychol. 2017 Jan. https://www.ncbi.nlm.nih.gov/pmc/articles/PMC5191916/

p.51 https://www.ncbi.nlm.nih.gov/books/NBK148970/#:~:text=FIGURE%205-,Oxytocin.,to%20get%20the%20milk%20easily.

p.72 https://www.sarawickham.com/articles-2/the-folly-of-fully-dilated/

p.75 Elizabeth C Aviv, Sofia I Cardenás, Gabriel León, Yael H Waizman, Cassin Gonzales, Genesis Flores, Magdalena Martínez-García, Darby E Saxbe. Prenatal prolactin predicts postnatal parenting attitudes and brain structure remodeling in first-time fathers. Psychoneuroendocrinology, Volume 156, 2023. https://www.sciencedirect.com/science/article/abs/pii/S0306453023003104

p.75 https://nationalpartnership.org/childbirthconnection/maternity-care/role-of-hormones/

p.75 https://www.aims.org.uk/journal/item/undisturbed-birth

p.77 Algoe SB, Kurtz LE, Grewen K. Oxytocin and social bonds: the role of oxytocin in perceptions of romantic partners' bonding behaviour. Psychol Sci. 2017 Dec. https://www.ncbi.nlm.nih.gov/pmc/articles/PMC5734372/

p.77 https://www.mindfulmamma.co.uk/the-power-of-love-birth-and-oxytocin/

p.77 Ito E, Shima R, Yoshioka T. A novel role of oxytocin: oxytocin-induced well-being in humans. Biophys Physicobiol. 2019 Aug. https://www.ncbi.nlm.nih.gov/pmc/articles/PMC6784812/

p.79 T Postel. Childbirth climax: the revealing of obstetrical orgasm. Sexologies, Volume 22, Issue 4. 2013. https://www.sciencedirect.com/science/article/abs/pii/S1158136013000467?via%3Dihub

p.79 https://www.britishjournalofmidwifery.com/content/literature-review/pain-and-pleasure-in-the-birthing-room-understanding-the-phenomenon-of-orgasmic-birth/

p.79 Beverly Whipple & Barry R Komisaruk (1988) Analgesia produced in women by genital self-stimulation, The Journal of Sex Research. 1986 Jun. https://www.tandfonline.com/doi/abs/10.1080/00224498809551403

p.82 Shojaei B, Loripoor M, Sheikhfathollahi M, Aminzadeh F. The effect of walking during late pregnancy on the outcomes of labour and delivery: A randomized clinical trial. J Educ Health Promot. 2021 Jul. https://www.ncbi.nlm.nih.gov/pmc/articles/PMC8395880/

p.83 Bowman, R, Taylor, J, Muggleton, S et al. Biophysical effects, safety and efficacy of raspberry leaf use in pregnancy: a systematic integrative review. BMC Complement Med Ther. 2021 Feb. https://bmccomplementmedtherapies.biomedcentral.com/articles/10.1186/s12906-021-03230-4

p.83 Al-Kuran O, Al-Mehaisen L, Bawadi H, Beitawi S, Amarin Z. The effect of late pregnancy consumption of date fruit on labour and delivery. J Obstet Gynaecol. 2011. https://pubmed.ncbi.nlm.nih.gov/21280989/

p.85 Abdolahian S, Ghavi F, Abdollahifard S, Sheikhan F. Effect of dance labour on the management of active phase labour pain and clients' satisfaction: a randomized controlled trial study. Glob J Health Sci. 2014 Mar. https://pubmed.ncbi.nlm.nih.gov/24762366/

p.86 Santiváñez-Acosta R, Tapia-López ELN, Santero M. Music therapy in pain and anxiety management during labour: a systematic review and meta-analysis. Medicina (Kaunas). 2020 Oct. https://www.ncbi.nlm.nih.gov/pmc/articles/PMC7599829/

p.88 https://www.yourhormones.info/hormones/relaxin/

p.90 https://mamastefit.com/opening-the-top-of-the-pelvis/

p.90 https://www.spinningbabies.com/pregnancy-birth/techniques/birth-balls

p.90 https://www.spinningbabies.com/pregnancy-birth/techniques/side-lying-release/

p.90 https://bodyreadymethod.com/pelvic-opening-during-pregnancy/

p.91 https://www.spinningbabies.com/pregnancy- birth/techniques/other-techniques/lunge/

p.91 https://macarthurmc.com/5-labour-positions-to-help-your-baby-come-out/

p.91 https://www.spinningbabies.com/optimal- maternal-postions-at-the-levels-of-the-pelvis/

p.92 DiFranco JT, Curl M. Healthy birth practice #5: avoid giving birth on your back and follow your body's urge to push. J Perinat Educ. 2014 Fall. https://www.ncbi.nlm.nih.gov/pmc/articles/PMC4235063/

p.94 https://n2physicaltherapy.com/pelvic-floor-and-the-jaw-whats-the-connection/

p.94 https://drlaurenkeller.com/

p.96 Issac A, Nayak SG, T P, Balakrishnan D, Halemani K, Mishra P, P I, Vr V, Jacob J, Stephen S. Effectiveness of breathing exercise on the duration of labour: A systematic review and meta-analysis. J Glob Health. 2023 Mar.

https://www.ncbi.nlm.nih.gov/pmc/articles/PMC9999308/

p.100 https://www.health.harvard.edu/mind-and-mood/endorphins-the-brains-natural-pain-reliever

p.102 Basu M, Smith D. Long-term outcomes of the Stop Traumatic OASI Morbidity Project (STOMP). Int J Gynaecol Obstet. 2018 Sep . https://pubmed.ncbi.nlm.nih.gov/29885253/

p.104 https://www.sciencedirect.com/topics/neuroscience/ferguson-reflex

p.104 Ahmadi Z, Torkzahrani S, Roosta F, Shakeri N, Mhmoodi Z. Effect of breathing technique of blowing on the extent of damage to the perineum at the moment of delivery: a randomized clinical trial. Iran J Nurs Midwifery Res. 2017 Jan–Feb. https://www.ncbi.nlm.nih.gov/pmc/articles/PMC5364755/

p.104 Joana Nunes Neta, Melania Maria Amorim, Julianna Guendler, Alexandre Delgado, Andréa Lemos, Leila Katz. Vocalization during the second stage of labour to prevent perineal trauma: a randomized controlled trial. European Journal of Obstetrics & Gynecology and Reproductive Biology, Volume 275, 2022. https://www.sciencedirect.com/science/article/abs/pii/S0301211522003839

p.104 https://www.ncbi.nlm.nih.gov/books/NBK539710/

p.116 Reitsma et al. Maternal outcomes and birth interventions among women who begin labour intending to give birth at home compared to women of low obstetrical risk who intend to give birth in hospital: a systematic review and meta-analyses. eClinical Medicine. 2020 Apr. https://www.thelancet.com/journals/eclinm/article/PIIS2589-5370(20)30063-8/fulltext

p.119 Burns E, Feeley C, Hall PJ, et al.

Systematic review and meta-analysis to examine intrapartum interventions, and maternal and neonatal outcomes following immersion in water during labour and waterbirth. BMJ Open 2022. https://bmjopen.bmj.com/content/12/7/e056517

p.119 https://www.sarawickham.com/research- updates/more-benefits-of-water-for-birth/

p.120 Reitsma et all (ibid).

p.122 Brigstocke S. MIDIRS Midwifery Digest, vol 24, no 2, 2014, pp 157–160

p.128 https://midwifethinking.com/2017/01/11/pre-labour-rupture-of-membranes-impatience-and-risk

p.130 Dahlen HG, Thornton C, Downe S, de Jonge A, Seijmonsbergen-Schermers A, Tracy S, Tracy M, Bisits A, Peters L. Intrapartum interventions and outcomes for women and children following induction of labour at term in uncomplicated pregnancies: a 16-year population-based linked data study. BMJ Open. 2021 May. https://pubmed.ncbi.nlm.nih.gov/34059509/

p.143 Tabatabaeichehr M, Mortazavi H. The effectiveness of aromatherapy in the management of labour pain and anxiety: a systematic review. Ethiop J Health Sci. 2020. https://www.ncbi.nlm.nih.gov/pmc/articles/PMC7445940/

p.145 https://www.ncbi.nlm.nih.gov/books/NBK542219/

p.145 Hiroaki Tanaka, Chizuko Kamiya, Shinji Katsuragi, Kayo Tanaka, Jun Yoshimatsu, Tomoaki Ikeda. Effect of epidural anesthesia in

labour; pregnancy with cardiovascular disease. Taiwanese Journal of Obstetrics and Gynecology. Volume 57, Issue 2. 2018. https://www.sciencedirect.com/science/article/pii/S1028455918300226

p.145 https://www.aims.org.uk/journal/item/epidurals-dead-from-the-waist-down

p.147 Kordi M, Irani M, Tara F, Esmaily H. The diagnostic accuracy of purple line in prediction of labour progress in Omolbanin Hospital, Iran. Iran Red Crescent Med J. 2014 Nov. https://www.ncbi.nlm.nih.gov/pmc/articles/PMC4329935/

p.152 Rabe H, Mercer J, Erickson-Owens D. What does the evidence tell us? Revisiting optimal cord management at the time of birth. Eur J Pediatr. 2022 May. https://www.ncbi.nlm.nih.gov/pmc/articles/PMC9056455/

p.153 https://midwifethinking.com/2015/03/11/an-actively-managed-placental-birth-might-be-the-best-option-for-most-women/

p.160 https://www.tommys.org/pregnancy-information/im-pregnant/early-pregnancy/how-common-miscarriage

p.160 https://www.tommys.org/baby-loss-support/pregnancy-loss-statistics

p.161 Pritchard S, Bianchi DW. Fetal cell microchimerism in the maternal heart: baby gives back. Circ Res. 2012 Jan 6. https://pubmed.ncbi.nlm.nih.gov/22223204/

p.161 Lim, G. Do fetal cells repair maternal hearts?. Nat Rev Cardiol 9, 67 (2012). https://doi.org/10.1038/nrcardio.2011.197

p.182 Beck CT, Watson S, Gable RK. Traumatic childbirth and its aftermath: is there anything positive? J Perinat Educ. 2018 Jun. https://pubmed.ncbi.nlm.nih.gov/30364308/

p.182 Hollander MH, van Hastenberg E, van Dillen J, van Pampus MG, de Miranda E, Stramrood CAI. Preventing traumatic childbirth experiences: 2192 women's perceptions and views. Arch Womens Ment Health. 2017 Aug. https://www.ncbi.nlm.nih.gov/pmc/articles/PMC5509770/

p.185 Prevost M, Zelkowitz P, Tulandi T, Hayton B, Feeley N, Carter CS, Joseph L, Pournajafi-Nazarloo H, Yong Ping E, Abenhaim H, Gold I. Oxytocin in pregnancy and the postpartum: relations to labour and its management. Front Public Health. 2014 Jan. https://www.ncbi.nlm.nih.gov/pmc/articles/PMC3902863/

p.196 https://www.lullabytrust.org.uk/safer-sleep-advice/co-sleeping

Further resources

Books

Spiritual Midwifery, Ina May Gaskin (Book Publishing Company, 2002)

Ina May's Guide to Childbirth, Ina May Gaskin (Vermillion, 2008)

Gentle Birth, Gentle Mothering, Sarah Buckley and Ina May Gaskin (Celestial Arts, 2009)

The Positive Birth Book, Milli Hill (Pinter & Martin, 2023)

Reclaiming Childbirth as a Rite of Passage, Rachel Reed (Word Witch, 2021)

The AIMS Guide to Your Rights in Pregnancy and Birth, Emma Ashworth (AIMS, 2020)

What's Right For Me?: Making decisions in pregnancy and birth (Birthmoon Creations, 2022) and *Plus Size Pregnancy: What the evidence really says about higher BMI and birth* (Birthmoon Creations, 2023), Dr Sara Wickham.

Mindful Hypnobirthing: Hypnosis and Mindfulness Techniques for a Calm and Confident Birth (Vermilion, 2019), Sophie Fletcher.

Websites

AIMS
www.aims.org.uk

Birth Rights.org
www.birthrights.org.uk

Birthing Instincts with Dr Stu and Dr Vic
www.birthinginstincts.com

Erin Fung
www.better-birth.co.uk

Evidence Based Birth®
www.evidencebasedbirth.com

Kemi Johnson
www.kemibirthjoyjohnson.com

NICE (The National Institute for Health and Care Excellence) www.nice.org.uk

Dr Rachel Reed
www.midwifethinking.com

Samantha Gadsden
www.caerphillydoula.co.uk

Dr Sara Wickham
www.sarawickham.com

Spinning Babies®
www.spinningbabies.com

The World Health Organization
www.who.int

Podcasts

The birth-ed Podcast
www.birth-ed.co.uk

Down To Birth Show
www.downtobirthshow.com

The Midwives' Cauldron
www.themidwivescauldron.buzzsprout.com

Welcome to the Womb

From the author

The Naked Birth App

The Naked Doula: Flashcards for Birth

The Visual Hypnobirth Programme

The Caesarean Birth Course

Index

Acknowledgments

Thank you Mum for always believing in me, and believing that I could do and be anything I wanted. For supporting me and letting me go rogue in all the ways I did. I wish you could see me now, I know how proud of me you'd be.

Thank you to my audience and followers for allowing me to share my work with you and be part of your stories. Your impact has meant I've been able to share even more with the world, and will continue to do so forever. Every single one of you has a part to play in my making and I appreciate you all. Thanks especially to those who have contributed their stories to this book.

To Megan, my agent for reaching out and making me feel super comfortable and confident. For supporting me and being the best advocate for my book deal and all the conversations we've had. You're amazing! I can always count on you to support all my choices, decisions and have unwavering confidence in me and my work. To Izzy and Jordan – what can I say? Thank you for challenging me throughout this journey. While you know I'm sure set on my work and how things should be, I am forever grateful for your passion in ensuring my work and book is portrayed as authentically as possible, in my voice and without fear. Sometimes this little old city girl can get carried away and you have continued to handle me with care, attention, and trust. Thank you to Bess and Satu as well, and to all of DK for the support.

Thank you Dad, for supporting me and spending pockets of time with my little George whilst I worked on this. Adam, for always being my biggest supporter and my two boys who continue to make me smile every single day. To Lisa, my mentor for keeping me on my path and Faye, my beautiful friend for being super special and always supporting me.

And finally, thank you to my primary school English teacher, Mr Alan Dapre for inspiring me to be an author!

About the author

Emma Armstrong, aka The Naked Doula, is a certified birth doula, hypnobirthing coach and birth influencer. Emma has turned her talent and experience as a professional and a mother into creating The Naked Doula, a centre for birth education that is both fun and engaging but most importantly fear-free. With online courses, masterclasses, flashcards, visual birth plans, The Naked Birth app, and in-labour support she reaches a wide community of women. As well as being a doula, Emma is an entrepreneur, writer, and illustrator. *The Fearless Birth Book* is her first book.

DK LONDON

Acquisitions Editor Becky Alexander
Project Editor Izzy Holton
Designer Jordan Lambley
Managing Editor Ruth O'Rourke
Senior Production Editor David Almond
Senior Production Controller Stephanie McConnell
Jacket and Sales Material Co-ordinator Emily Cannings
Editorial Director Elizabeth Neep
Art Director Maxine Pedliham
Publishing Director Katie Cowan

Editorial Satu Fox
Design Bess Daly

Publisher's Acknowledgment
DK would like to thank Dr Rachel Reed and Liadan Gunter for their help on consulting, Emma Ashworth for her contribution, Katie Crous for proofreading, and Lisa Footitt for indexing. DK would also like to thank Izzy Poulson for her design assistance, and Pushpak Tyagi for his technical support.

Disclaimer
The information in this book has been compiled by way of general guidance in relation to the specific subjects addressed. It is not a substitute and not to be relied on for medical, healthcare, pharmaceutical, or other professional advice on specific circumstances and in specific locations. Please consult your GP before starting, changing, or stopping any medical treatment. So far as the author is aware, the information given is correct and up to date as of December 2023. Practice, laws, and regulations all change, and the reader should obtain up-to-date professional advice on any such issues. The naming of any product, treatment, or organization in this book does not imply endorsement by the author or publisher, nor does the omission of any such names indicate disapproval. The author and publisher disclaim, as far as the law allows, any liability arising directly or indirectly from the use, or misuse, of the information contained in this book.

First published in Great Britain in 2024 by
Dorling Kindersley Limited
DK, One Embassy Gardens,
8 Viaduct Gardens,
London, SW11 7BW

The authorised representative in the EEA is Dorling Kindersley Verlag GmbH. Arnulfstr. 124, 80636 Munich, Germany

A CIP catalogue record for this book is available from the British Library.
ISBN: 978-0-2416-6873-3

Printed and bound in Slovakia

www.dk.com